18 STONES UP THE HILL

REMEMBRANCES OF A JOURNEYMAN CLUB CRICKETER

ANDREW KNOWLES

Copyright © ANDREW KNOWLES 2025
This book is sold subject to the condition that it shall not, by way of trade or otherwise, be lent, resold, hired out, or otherwise circulated without the publisher's prior consent in any form of binding or cover other than that in which it is published and without a similar condition including this condition being imposed on the subsequent publisher.
The moral right of ANDREW KNOWLES has been asserted.
ISBN: 978-1-0369-1288-8
Cover picture courtesy of Matthew Poole

This book is dedicated to the army of Club administrators, players, scorers, grass-cutters, groundsmen, sandwich and tea makers, bar stewards, umpires, coaches, juniors, and not forgetting the bloke who walks around the ground every Saturday with his 'lost ball' retrieving dog, without whom etc etc etc...

Also, to Dr Robert Waller
for his inestimable kindness, friendship and wisdom.

"Personally, I have always looked on cricket as organised loafing."

William Temple (1881-1944)

English theologian; Archbishop of Canterbury from 1942

CONTENTS

PREFACE 1
EARLY DAYS 3
SCHOOL YEARS 7
COUNTY MATCHES 15
ALBERT BRIAN JACKSON 27
BUXTON CC 30
WHEN SATURDAY COMES 43
PROPER CRICKET 46
OXFORD 61
WARMINSTER 75
UMPIRING 94
SOME OTHER PHOTOGRAPHS 103
ACKNOWLEDGEMENTS 107

18 STONES UP THE HILL

Remembrances of a journeyman club cricketer

Preface

I had been in the dressing room many times before, as a junior player or delivering the scorebook at the end of play, but be that as it may, the room took on a new dimension when first selected to play for a senior team.

It smelled different.

The floor, made up of lengths of two-foot-wide pieces of rubber conveyor belting, still had a hint of boiled cabbage about them, particularly when wet, but that hormonal B.O. of the juniors had been replaced by various fragrances emanating from aerosol cans or roll on deodorants. Adding to this olfactory minestrone the more seasoned, veteran members of the team might be applying a rub of Deep Heat or some other muscle relaxing salve, onto purposively stretched hamstrings or tensed calf muscles.

There also seemed to be a great improvement from junior days, in the aromas issuing forth from the various kit bags scattered about the room.

The odd towel might be hung up, perhaps not quite dry from Thursday nets, those of a certain age might have a body-bag or at least coat-hangers to keep tonight's courting kit neat and tidy. Some might do a last-minute boot whitening or another little ritual which always puzzled me; hair would be combed?

This was my introduction to the senior dressing room. A room familiar to sportsmen the world over. The bonding room, the room where instruction was taken and given, a room full of expectancy and anticipation.

You were in a man's world now, though perhaps only fourteen/fifteen years of age, where everybody showered openly, except perhaps Nobby Edge. That showering left the floor covered in images of feet, etched by talcum powder and looking like so many murder silhouettes.

Of course, at that age and totally innocent, I would have sat in the 'seen and not heard, speak when you're spoken to corner'. But taking it all in, listening to the banter, laughing when the others did, even if I hadn't a clue as to what the joke was about.

One of the first humorous stories I can remember and understand, not forgoing my tender years, was related in said dressing room just before turning out for Buxton CC second eleven, I'm guessing 1969/70ish.

It was often the case, as I would quickly learn, that sex would be a regular topic, not that I was as versed (then) *'dans les activités du boudoir'* as I hoped I might later become, but I knew enough to laugh. Anyway, one of our more esteemed members (a few years later he would be my boss) suggested that the team would perform better if everyone had sex on the Friday night, I would be sat in the corner head down but listening intently.

Another wag suggested what we needed was a new club 'bag'. (Cricket teams would have a club bag in those days to carry pads and bats, wicket keeping equipment etc.)

This was of course a pun on the word bag, as it might refer to a non-too- virtuous female.

Another member of the team, probably the eldest, a guy called Jack who wore bottle bottom thick glasses and tended to screw his face up when he spoke, announced to everyone; "Alright, alright, but I'm telling you this, if we do, I'm not going in number eleven."

EARLY DAYS

My very earliest memories were playing on the back lawn with dad. This wouldn't just be a knockabout; this would be very early coaching. He would always want me to 'play proper', showing me the correct way to stand and grip the bat. He used to instil in me that cricket was a sideways game, whether batting or bowling. He would always try to get me to hit the ball on the ground, 'you'll never be caught out if you hit it along the ground', was a much-repeated mantra. Although good and correct instruction, this probably had more to do with the proximity of windows, both ours and our neighbours.

I think of all the instruction I received from dad, the thing that stuck more than anything else was how to think about the game. He'd say, 'I'm going to get you out now', I would concentrate on stance and footwork, play a perfect forward defence, only to find he had delivered the tennis ball a yard shorter than all the others. I would connect with ball long after I should have done and usually up near the splice, the ball would gently spoon up into dad's hands. This would be the first of many lessons on line and length.

There were many other such sessions, either on the back lawn or beach, but looking back, what I believe the greatest lesson was, was to love the game. Dad instilled in me a respect and fascination for the game that I never lost and still have today - though I am less enamoured with the white ball game, particularly the very limited overs stuff. It reminds me of another lesson my father taught me, this time about beer. 'There's no bad beer son, but some's definitely better than others.'

My other vivid memory of cricket pre-secondary school would be at the home of my good friend Robert Waller. His house had a particularly accommodating back yard where many thousands of runs were scored. I'm sure we both achieved treble hundreds at one time or another. He also had a bright yellow, plastic cricket bat, which gave off a delightful 'thwack' if you caught it just right.

A lot of runs were scored with one of these.

Buxton Cricket Club play at The Park, Buxton.

Many of the substantial properties around The Park were built as the Devonshire Park Estate by none other than Joesph Paxton, great friend and Garden Designer to the Duke of Devonshire at Chatsworth House. Paxton had designed the magnificent Crystal Palace for the Great Exhibition of 1851.

Not only do I connect with Buxton and Warminster CC but, another great connection was forged by Sir Joseph Paxton. Whist working at Chatsworth as head gardener, Paxton developed the Cavendish Banana, which is the very same banana that we all know and love today, the one most widely eaten in the western world. That very same six-inches of deliciousness was imported by Geest into their Warminster Distribution Centre, in the millions.

At this time my family were wholly committed to Buxton Cricket Club, my mum would be on the teas roster, (this was great, it meant I got the crusts, not usually used), dad would umpire, both elder brothers would be playing and, in the old pavilion, I would be perched in the scorers' box, having climbed a very rickety ladder to the cramped room that was situated above the pavilion doors. Once seated at the table, the front would open out in two halves. The left-hand side would have a number of hooks screwed into it so that the home scorer, me, could hang the tins to show the score, wickets, last man etc. The tins were situated in a box on the floor and were double sided so, 1-2, 0-9 etc. The away scorer's half would have fewer hooks and would show the overs remaining if it was an overs match, and the bottom of his half would show the first innings score.

I loved scoring from a very early age. You were part of the team, and in the early days, there was no scoreboard facility to show individual scores, and there would be a particular thrill when a batsman neared a half-century, and you could inform his teammates watching below. The buzz if ever someone was approaching a century was electric.

Derek Morgan leads Derbyshire on to the field against Surrey at Buxton in 1964. The 'eyrie' scorebox can clearly be seen. There is a 50/50 chance the gentleman in the box is Andy Sandham.

(Courtesy Derbyshire. C.C.C. Archive.)

The vantage point this scorebox gave to a view over Buxton was superb. The Victorian Town Hall, styled after a French Chateau with a Mansard roof, clock tower and cupola stood proud on the skyline, and further down the vista between the Town Hall and cricket ground was the hotel whose sign confused many a visitor to the scorebox. The once impressive Spa Hotel had lost part of its P and from a distance looked like it might say the Sea Hotel. Well, I can tell you, it's a good walk to the beach from Buxton. The Spa Hotel was originally built in 1866 as an extension of the Malvern House Hydropathic, with an astonishing 260 rooms. In 1899 it was renamed the Buxton Hydropathic before becoming the Granville Military Hospital in WW1. In WW2 it became the offices and accommodation used by the evacuated Norwich Union Insurance Company. Becoming the Spa Hotel, it was demolished in 1973 for the development of Housing.

Dominating the view to the south are the forested sides of Grin Low hill, atop of which, at over 1400 feet, stands the Victorian folly that is known locally as Solomon's Temple.

Buxton has not always been blessed with the best of weather and enjoys(?) an average rainfall of 46.5 inches a year. Hence the saying, *'If you can see Solomon's Temple it's going to rain, if you can't see it...... it's raining.'*

SCHOOL YEARS

My secondary school years were nothing extraordinary but they were fun.

I went to what I thought was a good school for sport, I came from a very sporting family and would normally enjoy whatever came my way, though I must say the disciplines that included a lot of running would be avoided whenever possible. I was decent at cricket and rugby, and would be the well-built lad picked some way down the pecking order for the soccer elevens, (goalie usually, I filled it more than most of the other kids!). Athletics was never a great strength, but for the same reason I was never selected for running, I could throw a discus, or putt a shot.

Thinking back, the school had good sporting facilities. Two football pitches side by side and between them could be fashioned a fairly dodgy cricket pitch. A four-lane running track around the field could easily be accommodated, with a 100 yards straight running track cutting across the field. Two sandpits, one with a cinder track runway and both with dog excrement. *A good raking was always required before use.*

There were two rugby pitches as well, which were away from the school's own field, about a quarter of a mile's run away. (Or brisk walk!)

The school was divided into four Houses, Lansdowne, Marlborough, Sherwood and Curzon, *(I never knew why these names were selected, they were just four roads in the town?)* the school had a very competitive inter-house sports programme.

House matches in whichever sport, or the Olympian Sports Day were a big thing and rivalries were often fierce, but whatever the outcome, you could read about each and every match, in the monthly edition of **'Sport'** - the school magazine that covered every sporting activity. With the occasional Quiz or Crossword and most importantly reports of Inter-Schools matches, the magazine was a monthly must. As captain in Rugby and Cricket I used to love writing up the reports for the **'Sport'**.

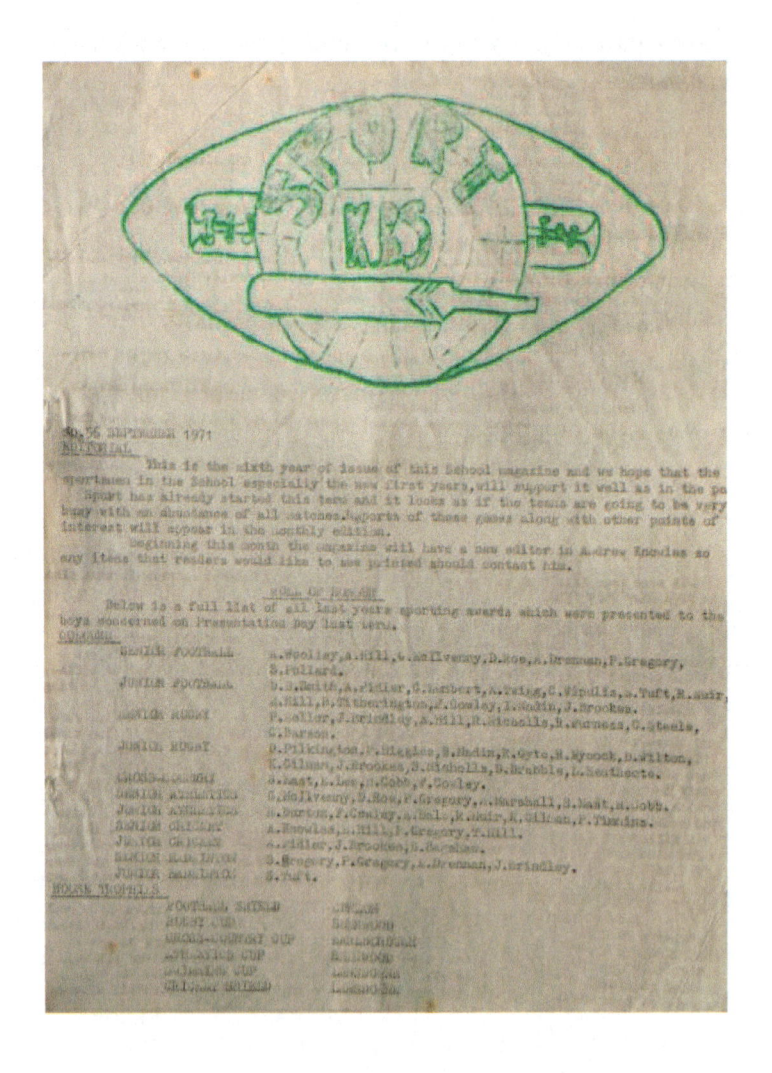

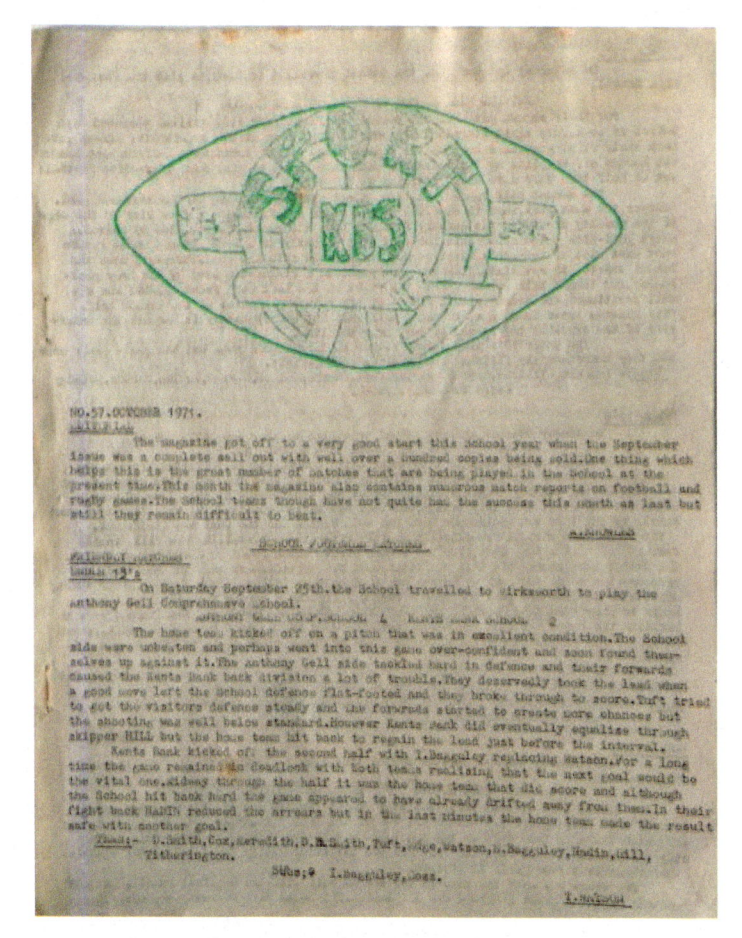

A New Editor, An early edition.

Picture courtesy Andrew Drennan.

The school I attended was a boy's Secondary Modern School named Kents Bank. The town also had a Sec Mod school for girls called Silverlands and two grammar schools, Cavendish for the girls and Buxton College for the lads. The College also had boarders.

I was lucky to have a sports master at my school who was a keen local cricketer, I was even more fortunate that he had a brother of my age at a similar school just down the road in Chapel-en-le Frith.

It was this schoolmaster who got hold of the information that there were going to be trials for Derbyshire Schoolboys U16s to be held in Chesterfield, ten days or so hence.

I say "got hold of the information" because I remember him telling me that the school had had no official notification, and that he'd had to make a number of phone calls to get myself and his brother to attend as trialists.

I don't think secondary schools like ours were on the radar of such august organisations as the Selection Panel for the Schoolboys County Cricket Teams.

Anyway, we went, we trialled, we got selected.

The first big thrill of being selected was to attend a weekend coaching camp at, what was in those days, the Derbyshire Centre of Sporting Excellence - Lea Green. (Scoff you not! I'll have you know that none other than the squad of the 1966 World Cup winners trained and stayed at the Lea Green complex in 1964 - It might even have been where Sir Alf worked out the transitional system which allowed him to switch from 4-4-3 to 4-3-1-2 two years later. Well, it might have ...)

In our case the coaching for the weekend was directed by Mr Eric Marsh, a man who I'd vaguely heard of as an ex-Derbyshire cricketer but knew little or nothing of apart from that.

(Eric Marsh in fact played 66 matches for Derbyshire taking 44 wickets and scoring 1698 runs. At the time of my Lea Green visit he was the cricket coach at Repton School.)

I have to say, that of the weekend from a cricketing point of view, nothing much is memorable, it might have been the first time I'd experienced indoor nets, but other than that, not a lot.

Lea Green - as it is today.
Picture by kind permission Lea Green Administration.

On the social side though, good friendships were made, particularly by those of us who had already started to enjoy a pint. One of our number, a lad named Mick Glenn, who went on to play half a dozen games for Derbyshire, (one of which was the infamous 1975 match at Buxton) was about 6ft 7in even then, and so when we wandered into the village to the Jug and Glass public house, we had no difficulty in getting a pint. We were sat there minding our own business when two or three of the staff or 'selectors' walked in. I think it was only the presence of Mick, of whom they had high hopes, that stopped the rest of us being sent home.

I was taken to one side later that afternoon, where it was suggested to me that the Jug and Glass was not the place for a Derbyshire U16 cricketer to be seen. I think mention was also made of the fact that by then I was on about 30 Bensons a day, this behaviour just wouldn't do at all. The simple conclusion was, I just wasn't cut out to be a chap...

Perhaps I was the very epitome of why schools like mine didn't get an invite in the first place.

We had a week's cricket against other counties. We never travelled too far and I actually remember very little of it, other than I think we lost every game. I was only selected for one match, which was against Notts and played at Spondon. I recall not one delivery of my bowling or batting that day, probably because there was nothing worth remembering.

What I do recall, was the blatant, conspicuous and shameless cheating by the umpires who were all made up of staff members from the respective counties. So obvious was it, that people were desperate to bowl at the end of their 'own' umpire. We were only young schoolkids but we could see what was going on. I suspect that not one batsman was given out L.B.W. by his 'own' umpire, but that won't have mattered as plenty will have been given out by the other one.

The hypocrisy of being told, 'you're a very naughty boy' by the very same people who would shamelessly cheat all day when umpiring was not lost on me, I decided I didn't want to be a chap.

Thus ended my days of representative cricket. If anybody ever writes a history of Derbyshire schoolboy cricket I doubt very much that great heaps of lavish praise will pour down on my head, I most certainly won't get a mention unless there is a chapter titled, 'Rogues Gallery'. I do remember some weeks after, 'his achievements at representing the school' being broadcast by the Headmaster at morning assembly, where I was invited up on to the stage to be presented with a Derbyshire Schoolboys tie.

In my formative years, if you wanted to know about sport, and I did, you read newspapers.

Computers were still science fiction, there were boxes with flashing lights on Doctor Who, but only the good Doctor himself had access to these.

We had only three TV channels (and none of them came on till tea-time). There were no sports channels, the only live football matches shown would be the F.A.Cup Final and the annual Home internationals. On Saturday afternoons the BBC had Grandstand and ITV had World of Sport. This was really world of non-sport, full of things like wrestling, moto-cross and water-ski jumping. The Beeb had the proper sport like cricket, rugby league and union, horse racing and the brilliant football scores service where everyone tried to guess the result by the intonation of how the reader said the first team and score.

There was one midweek round up sports programme, David Coleman's Sportsnight, where if you were very lucky you might catch the odd glimpse of a goal scored in club football.

So, if you wanted to know, it was newspapers or nothing.

My father, God rest his soul, took the Daily Mail every day, (and I've only just forgiven him!) I think most, if not all the daily papers back then would print the county cricket scores. I would devour them, reading every scorecard of every game, every day. When the newspapers had been consumed, I would almost always have a cricket book on the go.

'Spinning round the World' by Jim Laker, Ritchie Benaud's 'A Tale of Two Tests', Cricketers' Cricket by Sir Learie Constantine, a book I still have. There would be well thumbed editions of old Wisdens, Derbyshire Year Books and The Cricketer magazine, many read and re-read, an insatiable thirst for all things cricket.

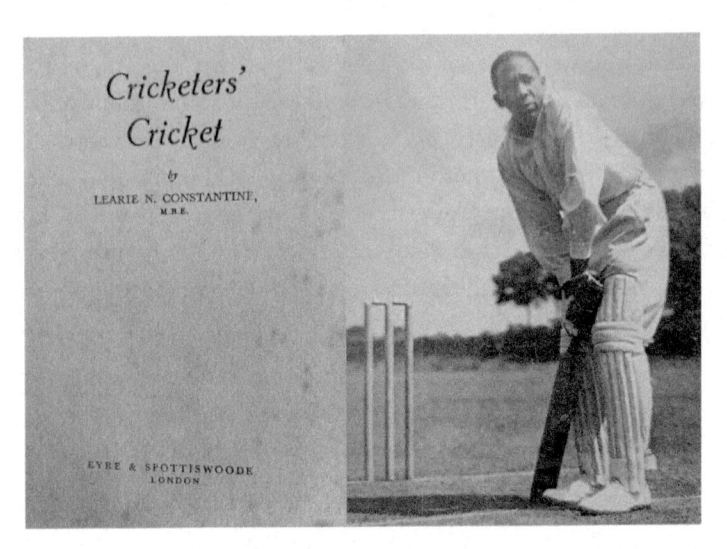

Sir Learie Constantine.

COUNTY MATCHES

I recall with immense pride being gifted two days off school by our headmaster whose name was Jack Curtis. In those early teen years cricket meant everything to me, as yet there were very few other distractions on the horizon. Every year Buxton Cricket Club would be awarded a home County Championship cricket match for Derbyshire CCC. This was the highlight of my year; my heroes were coming to town.

The Major Domo of Buxton CC was a loud and imposing man, with a military disposition, he might well have been an actual major, his name was Jim Pettman and his voice would boom across the ground, you could never fail to know you were in his presence. Anyway, his younger son Roger and I would cut the grass, the outfield, for the club, but come county match time this required a certain amount of precision as the ground needed to be striped.

It was Jim Pettman who had contacted Jack Curtis, the headmaster at my school, asking if I might be excused for a couple of days for this vital work required at the ground.

So, two or three days prior to the match, Roger and I would watch enthusiastically as Jim, wheeling a barrowful of old stumps onto the ground would take a handful. He would deliberately pace out 14 steps and stick a stump in the ground. He would then walk the length of the ground, parallel to the pitch, sticking another stump in every 30 yards or so, keeping the line as straight as the eye would allow. Measuring fourteen paces towards the square another line of accurately placed stumps would shadow the first, repeating this process two or three more times, so there were perhaps four or five lines of stumps marching in a straight line, the length of the ground. I would start the big sit-on mower at the boundary edge, mow to the top, turn left and come back down the other side of the first line of stumps. At the same time, Roger would get on the other sit-on mower, usually borrowed from Jim's school, (he was the Bursar at the adjacent Public School, Normanton) and proceed in the same direction up the left-hand side of the second line of stumps, turning at the top and repeating. When we had reached to final row of stumps, Jim who by now had collected the first three rows of stumps, would march across the ground, inserting the next rows for Roger and I to follow, this would be repeated until the entire ground was beautifully striped.

What great days, definitely better than school, thank you Jack Curtis, thank you Jim Pettman.

The days of the annual county match were my halcyon days, the Blue Remembered Hills of 'my' youth. Weeks of excited anticipation, hours of mowing grass that hadn't been mown since last year's game, I even recall using a scythe to tackle the really long grass by the Park Road entrance, finding lost cricket balls, we'd usually have a few extra net balls by the end of the mowing.

The wooden sight-screens we had, normally one at each end would be freshly whitewashed, and the one normally at the bottom of the ground, would, with some difficulty, be pushed to the pavilion end to form a double screen as in the picture below. Temporary screens, some kind of canvas or white sheeting would be erected at the bottom end of the ground.

The boundary edge had bench seating around about two thirds of its length and nailed to the back of this seating were lengths of the same conveyor belt material that covered the dressing room floor. (*The club must have had a very good contact for disused conveyor belting*).

This fell into disrepair and for a few years, prior to the County Match, there would be efforts to re-affix it but the Buxton winters did little to preserve either seating or belting and in the end it was a lost cause.

As can be seen in the picture below, the pavilion sat atop a banked area some way above the level of playing field. From boundary edge to pavilion, two flights of steps had to be negotiated, these made from old railway sleepers. This height or mound gave the ground an amphitheatre effect at the pavilion end and the seating on it gave the best view of the cricket possible.

*The Park Buxton - A County Match from the mid-sixties.
Picture courtesy Derbyshire C.C.C. archive.*

On the first morning of any county match, whatever we were doing, every minute would be a fresh look towards the car park hoping to get that first glimpse of this year's famous cricketers who were coming to play at 'your' ground.

In no particular order, I remember the then household names such as; John Edrich, Brian Statham, Dennis Amiss, MJK Smith, Tom Cartwright, Greg Chappell - he had the neatest autograph I ever got - Farokh Engineer. At close of play we would sneak into the dressing rooms to look at the player's kit. Farokh had the lightest cricket bat imaginable - Clive Lloyd - the heaviest bat and thickest handle -, John Snow, Tony Greig, Graham Hick. Gracing the Derbyshire badge included, Eddie Barlow, Alan Ward, Mike Hendrick, Lawrence Rowe, John Wright, Michael Holding and of course, Srinivasaraghaven Venkataraghavan, not unsurprisingly known the world over as Venkat.

One of the many tasks given to we younger members was the stocking and daily re-stocking of the beer tents each morning. I didn't yet really know pubs, but after only one day, the tents would have that lovely boozy, smoky fug about them that became lost with the banning of smoking. I don't really miss the cigarettes, but the pubs were never as homely and inviting after the smoking ban.

I recall lugging crates of big bottles of lemonade, these were heavy and glass, two people to a crate. The fun of rolling kegs down the path from the pavilion to the club's tea hut, which served as one bar, or further to the large marquee, erected on what have since become tennis courts. A further tent was situated just below the pavilion to the right a few yards past the scoreboard. As I recall these times one other memory has me salivating like Homer Simpson. Often, the early bird workers, of which my brothers and I might be some, would pile into Mr Burgess's or Mr Cockram's car and head to Vale's Cafe on West Road for a delicious bacon butty, pure joy.

What of the cricket? Well, there were county championship matches at The Park, every year in an unbroken run (Apart from WW2) from 1930- 1976, the County Championship returned in 1980 and again in 1984/5/6.

A shot from, I'm guessing, a county match late 70's early 80's. It looks like Jack Simmons at 2nd slip, perhaps Frank Hayes at 1st slip and that could be Bumble Lloyd at mid-on. Just a guess, I can't confirm it. Picture courtesy Derbyshire CCC Archive.

However, the first recorded first-class match took place in June 1923 when Derbyshire entertained the visiting West Indies tourists. Perhaps the pitch was a tad green as the W.I. were 97a.o. in their first innings, of which Mr, later Sir, later Lord Learie Constantine scored 60 n.o.

My very first memory was from August 1964 when I would have been just short of my ninth birthday. Hanging around the pavilion with my autograph book, my father, who always worked behind the pavilion bar during the county match, took me to one side. He pointed at a quite distinguished, elderly, trilby-hatted gentleman, sat quietly on his own and enjoying a post day's play cup of tea. Go and ask that man for his autograph, my father prompted. I did as I was told, much to the amusement of the gentleman. 'Do you know who I am'? he asked smiling. I had to admit that I didn't but hastily added, 'My dad does', the gentleman signed my book in beautiful copperplate script. I rushed back over to dad, 'who is it' I asked. Teasingly, dad replied, 'you'll have to look him up back home'.

Later, after tea, dad told me to fetch my autograph book, 'now' he said, reaching for a book of cricket records we had, 'what did the gentleman write?' I looked at the book, 'Andy Sandham?' I replied, none the wiser. With that my father passed me the book and told me to, 'see if you can find him in there'.

I did find him and was amazed to read, that the man who had signed my autograph book, scored the first ever triple century in Test Cricket history. At Kingston Jamaica in 1930 Andy Sandham scored 325 against the West Indies. He was now the Surrey CCC scorer.

(In the 1972 Wisden, Andy Sandham wrote an illuminating article about his time in cricket. It gives a fascinating insight in to the game between the two great wars and in particular what it was like to bat with Jack Hobbs.)

Another tale of those times that I loved to hear my dad tell, and he never tired of telling it, was when again he was behind the bar.

This was the match in 1960 and Derbyshire were hosting Sussex. One afternoon my father was approached by a very dapper looking young man dressed in whites and wearing a colourful blazer. Tapping his blazer pockets to indicate to my father that he had no money on him, the young man asked dad if he would 'stand' him a book of matches until after play had finished. Dad thought long and hard, a ha'penny was a ha'penny but, being the kind man he was dad risked it and gave the young man his matches. Dad used to revel in saying that this wasn't such a risk after all, as the young man in question was the Nawab of Pataudi.

(When I was very young my dad used to tell me, he played in the game where somebody hit the cricket ball 82 miles. I would sit open mouthed as he told me of a match, he was playing in in Ambergate, a village between Derby and Matlock. A batsman hit the ball for six but it landed in a railway wagon that was passing and was found the next day in York.)

Another vivid recollection I have came in the County Match of 1968, Derbyshire v Somerset, I would be almost 13 years old. I was approached by a guy I had seen come out of the press tent; somebody must have recommended me to him.

'Is it Andrew?' he asked walking towards me.

'Yes,' I replied, not knowing the man from Adam.

'Would you like to do a big favour for Harold Rhodes?'

Would I, I thought, of course I would.

'Yes OK,' I said.

He then went on to explain that his name was Mike Carey and that he was the editor of the Harold Rhodes Testimonial Book, he went on to ask me if I would walk around the ground, each day, selling said books.

So, with an armful of books, I walked right around the ground, once in the morning, during the lunch break, in the afternoon, during the tea interval and finally just before close of play, happily chirping, 'Harold Rhodes Testimonial Books 2/6, Harold Rhodes Testimonial Books 2/6.

That sales went really well was not hindered by a splendid

performance from the home team. Batting first Derbyshire reached 400 for 4 before declaring, with centuries from Mike Page and Derek Morgan. Then, just before close of play, Harold bowled the Somerset opener, Roy Virgin for just 5 runs.

On the second day Derbyshire put in a splendid performance in the field, bowling Somerset out for 179, Rhodes taking 3 for 26 and Brian Jackson finishing with 4 for 41. Enforcing the follow on, Rhodes again nipped out a Somerset opener before close of play, this time Mervyn Kitchen - later a most distinguished Test Match umpire - caught behind by Bob Taylor for 26.

Somerset made a better fist of their second innings reaching 296 before being bowled out, Harold Rhodes taking 4 for 57. Derbyshire almost ended up throwing away what should have been an easy victory. Needing only 76 to win they stumbled over the line, reaching the required 76 for the loss of 8 wickets. This was mainly due to a fine spell of fast bowling by Fred Rumsey, who took 4 for 30.

Fred Rumsey played for Worcestershire, Somerset and England but would end his career at Derbyshire, where he played one-day cricket from 1969-73. He also operated as chief fund raiser and Public Relations Officer for the county. Fred Rumsey, in 1967, also founded the PCA, the Professional Cricketers Association.

As you can imagine it was a good week for selling the books, a Derbyshire win, Harold involved all the way through - even getting a 0* red inker at the death - everybody seemed very happy.

I think I was paid 3d per book sale, I can't remember how many I sold but I do recall feeling quite flush after receiving payment, it was a good earner for a twelve-year-old.

No doubt this experience was good training for a future career in sales.

Mike Carey paid up and then asked me to follow him up to the pavilion. He went inside and then a couple of minutes later came out with Harold himself who thanked me profusely for what I had done and then produced from behind his back a brand-new cricket jumper, which he presented me with. I think at that moment in my tender years it was the happiest I had ever been.

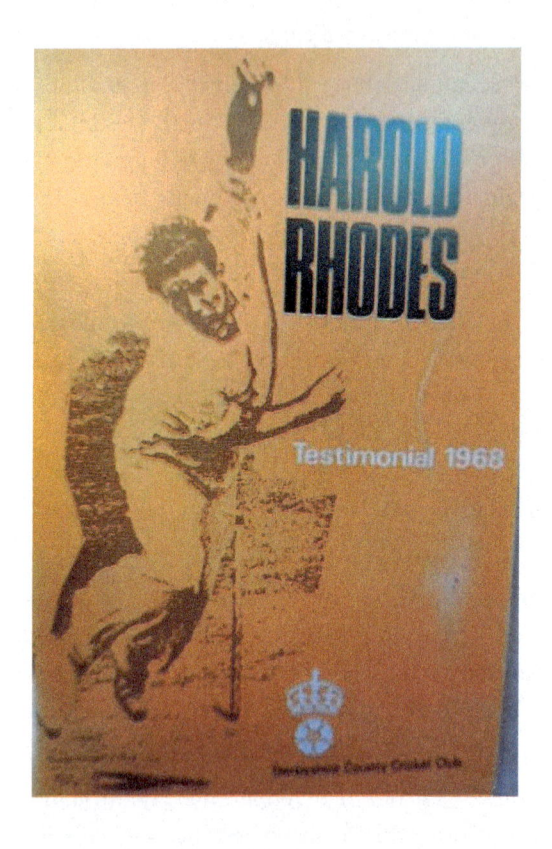

HAROLD RHODES Testimonial 1968

While the most common and obvious first-class visitors to The Park were Lancashire, who have made the short journey from Old Trafford 26 times, the Derbyshire faithful have also witnessed visits from, Leics, Sussex, Glos, Kent, Middx, Essex, Worcs, Northants, Somerset and Warks. In addition to these, Derbyshire hosted Ireland in 1947, Scotland in 1954 and Oxford Uni in 1961.

In addition to these first-class games, Derbyshire also played a total of 10 Sunday League fixtures, initially the John Player County League, then the John Player league. (Subsequently other sponsors took over.) These fixtures ran consecutively from 1969-76 then one in 1980 and a final one in 1986.

An unforgettable memory for a lad of an impressionable age is of the very attractive John Player girls, bedecked in a uniform of short skirt, blouse and JPS sash, carrying before them an usherette's box of John Player goodies, if was enough to make you want to start smoking!!!

The only county not in the previous list to visit Buxton for a Sunday League game was Glamorgan, firstly in 1973 and then in the middle of the most infamous county match we ever had, 1975.

The 3-day game, against Lancashire started on Saturday 31st May and as always a healthy crowd basked in the early summer sunshine. A glorious day weather wise and an even better one cricket wise, particularly if you were a Lancashire fan. The Red Rose County amassed a staggering total of 477 off their 100 overs, highlight of which was the highest first class score ever made on The Park, 167 n.o. by one Clive Lloyd. One old boy seated near me watched one of Clive's sixes climb and climb ever further into the sky and way out of the ground, 'that bugger'll have snow on it when it comes down,' he said, how prophetic. Frank Hayes also scored a century and there were 50s for Bumble Lloyd and Jack Simmons. By close of play on that first day Derbyshire had reached 25 for 2.

Come the Sunday, weather still fine, Derbyshire bat first against Glamorgan and in their 40 overs scored 215 for 6, almost half of them scored by Ron Headley who hit 95. In reply, Glamorgan scored 187, Derbyshire winning by 28 runs.

How times change, these days 215 would be just about a par T20 score!

Monday morning arrives and the Derbyshire and Lancashire teams reassemble, to watch it rain. There is a distinct nip in the air and before very long the rain turns to hail. What happened next was pictured across the front pages of most of the nationals the next day. About an inch of snow, this was June 2nd! Not surprisingly there was no play on day two of the match.

Day three was at least dry overhead and the umpires, one Harold - Dickie - Bird and one Albert - Dusty - Rhodes declared it playable.

It didn't last long; Derbyshire were shot out for 42 on what was now a seriously dodgy pitch to bat on. Peter Lever, the Lancashire and England opening bowler refused to bowl fast on it, not wishing to hurt anyone. I'm guessing not a lot of consideration or hand wringing was required for David Lloyd to decide to enforce the follow on.

This time round Derbyshire doubled their first inning score to reach 87 before being all out. Equal top scorers for Derbyshire were Alan Morris and Ashley Harvey-Walker with 26 apiece. Ashley Harvey-Walker amused the crowd by, as he walked into bat, approaching the square leg umpire, taking a handkerchief from his pocket and wrapping his false teeth in it before passing them to the umpire for safe keeping.

So, a game that lasted shorter than two days ended in a win for Lancashire by an innings and 348 runs. That must be some kind of record in itself. All of this preceded one of the longest, hottest summers those of us old enough can remember.

The following weekend, a photographer from the nationals turned up and photographed a bunch of us Buxton cricketers basking in the glorious sunshine. One of the papers, The Daily Express or Mail, I can't remember which, printed a before/after, last week/this week picture in their Monday edition.

What I can't for the life of me remember is whether or not the pitch got covered. I just don't recall, though the way the game went suggests not. I know covers started being used in first class cricket in the sixties, though whether they were mandatory or not I don't know, and there was also a time when only the wicket ends were covered, maybe this was one of those times. I'd be happy for someone to solve this for me.

An interesting aside to this is that the two umpires stood in both the 3 day and the Sunday League games. Though not playing in the 3-day game Harold Rhodes did bowl for Derbyshire in the Sunday fixture and AEG 'Dusty' Rhodes was his father. Imagine turning to the umpire and appealing loudly 'howzat dad'. This probably never happened, I'm guessing that Harold would always bowl at Dickie Bird's end.

Though I can imagine it's happened in the odd Buxton CC club game at The Park, ahem....

A sad footnote to end on here: In 1997, in a bar in Johannesburg, a man walked in and called out Ashley Harvey-Walkers name and when Ashley responded, the man shot him dead.

In 2023 I was also saddened to read of the death of Mike Carey. Mike had a long and distinguished career as a journalist for the Daily Telegraph amongst others, he was also an author and radio presenter on Radio Derby. I believe at one time he also edited the Stoke City fan-magazine the Clipper, or to give it its full name the Ceramic City Clipper. After the Harold Rhodes books I would see Mike every year at the county match, he would always speak and have time for you, as I got older, the conversations would always be more interesting and enlightening.

R.I.P Mike.

There were many happy times and incidents that took place at or during the county match each year.

One of the occasions I missed for some unknown reason, so this is hearsay, was when Test Match umpire David Constant adjudicated on the veracity of the bowling action of the Buxton College Latin master, and Buxton CC 2nd XI stalwart, known universally as Snave. (See Oxford)

This would have been sometime during the 1974 county match against Lancashire or the Sunday League match against Warwickshire.

Mr Evans (Snave) had quite possibly downed a Stingo or three but, as I understand it, the bowling green floodlights were turned on and England's premier umpire adjudicated his action from a position akin to square leg. To this day I don't know what the judgement was.

(If anyone who ever reads this can fill me in in greater detail as to what happened I would be grateful and happy to amend.)

Another humorous tale I recall from those times was regarding the West Indian cricketer Elquemedo Tonito Willett, not a household name and a man who only played in 5 test matches. How this story came about I'm unsure, it had absolutely nothing to do with the county match that was taking place. I think it emanated from the press box, perhaps during a quiet spell in the play. However, a group of friends and I were told that the said cricketer was blessed with the most enormous member anyone had ever seen. So big was it, it was said, that even some of the other West Indian cricketers preferred to shower either before or after Elquemedo Tonito Willett.

This story has nothing whatsoever to do with my cricket journey, but it always rather amused me.

ALBERT BRIAN JACKSON

Albert Brian Jackson. Picture courtesy Derbyshire C.C.C. archive.

As I was putting the finishing touches to this bit of fun I received news that was anything but, I was informed that Albert Brian Jackson had passed away on 26/11/2024.

Better qualified and more illustrious people than me will write about Brian, but from the bottom of my heart I can only say what a privilege it was to have played with him and known him as a friend.

'Never meet your heroes, they'll surely disappoint' as the saying goes, you would hate to find they had 'feet of clay'.

Well not Jacko, not one bit of it.

From my earliest days playing junior cricket when he was our non-playing captain, right through to my last ever game with him - which was I don't know when - what emanated from Brian was nothing but pure enthusiasm. I'll bet Brian got as much pleasure from taking his last wicket as he got from say, taking the wicket of the world's best batsman at the time, Graeme Pollock or that of

Geoffrey Boycott, both of which he did dismiss. He was so encouraging to play with, if you took a wicket Brian would be as pleased for you as he would be for himself.

I'll never forget the groan that would emanate from him if someone played a bad shot off him and got four, or worse, a Chinese Cut, he hated that. Even if it was at the end of his career when he was bowling (very flat) off breaks you could guarantee the next one would be a bit quicker.

He played for Derbyshire from 1963-1968 in total 149 first class matches, during which he took 457 wickets.

In the 1965 season, Brian finished second in the first-class averages to none other than his good mate and opening partner Harold Rhodes.

Harold's season's analysis was:

646.2 overs, 187 maidens, 1314 runs, 119 wkts, at an average of 11.04

Jacko's season's analysis was:

807.5* overs, 262 maidens, 1491 runs, 120 wkts, at an average of 12.42

You might think that they would have been a shoo-in for England honours but just consider, in the same season Brian Statham off 771 overs took 137/1716 at an average of 12.52, and Fred Trueman off 754 overs took 127/1811 at an average of 14.25. In addition to these great bowlers, Fred Rumsey, David Brown and Ken Higgs were all pushing for England caps. It would be true to say that the country was blessed with pace bowling talent in that era.

*808 overs in one season, some of today's quick bowlers can't get through a T20 series without breaking down.

After he'd finished at Derbyshire, he played most of his club cricket at Buxton and I think the odd game for Cheshire.

ABJ was great company, you could not be in his presence very long without laughing. A memorable evening was spent in his and

David Green's company in Vincent's Club in Oxford.

We had bumped into David in The Parks where he was reporting on the University match for the Daily Telegraph and Jacko had suggested we meet for light refreshment later on.

David Green would be contemporary to Jacko but as a top order batsman for Lancashire, later Gloucestershire amassing 13,381 first class runs in the process.

Jacko would offer, 'I poled you that day in Blackpool with a little nipper backer'. 'Aye', David would respond, 'But not before I'd got 50'.

It was 'Wisdens' at 20 paces, great fun.

One of the most memorable things I remember Jacko saying and it makes me smile to think of it now:

'I used to bowl two bad balls a year, one in April when I wa' stiff and one in September when a wa' tired'.

R.I.P Brian.

BUXTON CC

Junior cricket went well, the Buxton Juniors played in the Derbyshire and Cheshire Junior League. This was a good league with some very good clubs in it. I used to envy the fact that D&C clubs had so many 'derby' fixtures, whereas Buxton had none. Most of the league would have been within a ten-mile radius of New Mills and the best players in each club would have been well known by everyone else. This must have made for some fiery and hard-fought fixtures, particularly with the clubs being so close and some players moving teams from year to year. A lot of fixtures must have had a touch of spice added to them.

Buxton Juniors managed to win the league a couple of times during my playing days. We had some very good young cricketers, and were helped immensely by having A.B. Jackson as the non-playing captain. An interesting concept - the non-playing skipper - it's a bit like having your wife in the car while you're driving.

Some years later in the early 80's, Peter 'Gaffer' Hardman and I decided to do our cricket coaching badges.

So, in the spring of 1983, Gaffer would collect me at 9.00 on a Sunday morning and off we'd trundle in 'Hawkwind' (Gaffer and his wife Robyn's much loved VW Campervan) down to the County Ground at Derby. The course was very comprehensive and made most enjoyable by our instructor, one Percy Bown. (I do hope I've remembered his name properly - it wasn't Brown if that's what you're thinking.)

Percy was very enthusiastic, such a great quality in teachers, and he made every Sunday morning most enjoyable.

None more so than the week we turned up to do wicket-keeping, for there, stood at the side of Percy, was none other than Bob Taylor. Regarded by a lot of people as the finest wicket-keeper of his generation but perhaps not the finest wicket-keeper/batsman. Nevertheless, he played 639 first class matches for Derbyshire and

57 games for England, and who can forget his fantastic contribution in the '81 Ashes series, pouching four of Bob Willis's eight wickets in the famous Headingly victory, and taking a great catch to dismiss Dennis Lillee in the famous triumph at Edgbaston, just 10 days later, where Ian Botham had that amazing spell of 5 for 1.

We stood mouth agape but listening intently as Bob almost nonchalantly collected balls thrown hard from a shortish distance, describing what to be looking for, picking up length, staying low, being on the balls of your feet so you could move to the left or right with ease. It was an absolute masterclass from an absolute master.

At the end of the course 10 or 12 weeks, we had to sit a written exam that was quite exhaustive, nevertheless, we both passed and we both got one of these, though I've lost mine!

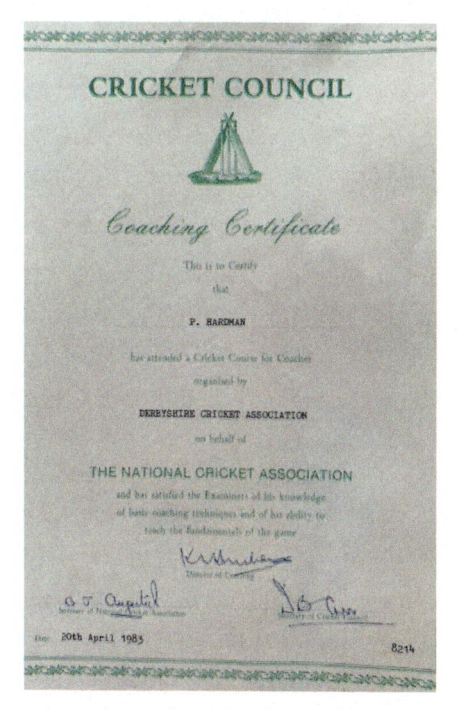

With grateful thanks to Robyn.

This from the Buxton Advertiser May 1987.
With grateful thanks to Geoff Needham.

Whilst we are on the subject of Hawkwind', it would be remiss not to mention a cricketing escapade that Gaffer, myself and our great friend Andrew 'Panjo' Drennan embarked on in June 1979.

We trundled off, at no great speed this was Hawkwind after all, to the beautiful Cotswold village of Bisley, where by prearrangement, we parked up overnight in the car park of the Stirrup Cup pub. This happened to be the favourite watering hole of my eldest brother Cec.

One unusual thing about the evening we enjoyed in the Stirrup Cup was that someone came in the pub with a fox on a lead. The story was that the fox, as a cub, was the only survivor of a gas attack that wiped the rest of the earth or skulk. This cub had been brought up with some dog pups and was almost totally domesticated. It jumped up onto the bench by its master and rested his head on his knee just as a dog might.

The next morning it was off to Cardiff for the quarter final of that years Benson and Hedges Cup between Glamorganshire and Derbyshire.

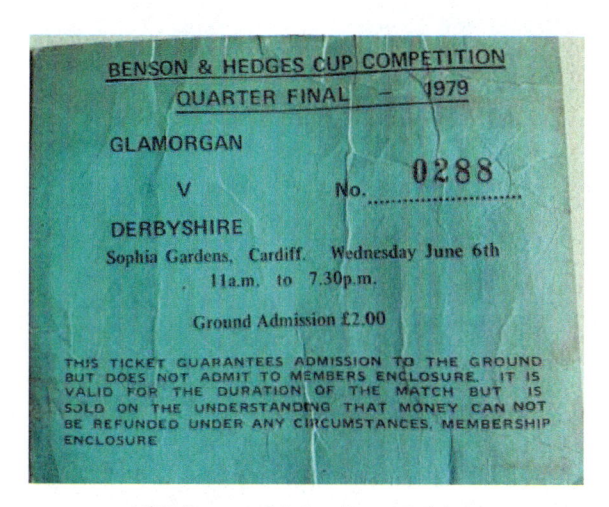

```
BENSON & HEDGES CUP COMPETITION
       QUARTER FINAL -    1979
   GLAMORGAN
           V         No.   0288
   DERBYSHIRE
       Sophia Gardens, Cardiff.  Wednesday June 6th
                   11a.m. to 7.30p.m.
              Ground Admission £2.00
    THIS TICKET GUARANTEES ADMISSION TO THE GROUND
    BUT DOES NOT ADMIT TO MEMBERS ENCLOSURE. IT IS
    VALID FOR THE DURATION OF THE MATCH BUT IS
    SOLD ON THE UNDERSTANDING THAT MONEY CAN NOT
    BE REFUNDED UNDER ANY CIRCUMSTANCES, MEMBERSHIP
    ENCLOSURE
```

With grateful thanks to Robyn.

A great win for the Rams ensued, Glamorgan reached 197/5 in their 55 overs, and in reply Derbyshire knocked the runs off for the loss of 4 wickets in 51.3 overs. Our Kiwi John Wright scored 101 and Buxworth lad Bud Hill scored 44.

When you look back at the scores of early limited overs cricket, they really are paltry to what one can expect now, again the above scores might be a T20 game these days.

The next couple of nights were spent, firstly in Warminster on brother Chas's drive, and then in Winchester at relatives of Gaff's.

The Friday night we found a space in Staines next to the Thames, it being our intention to go to Lords the next day to try and see England and Australia in the 1979 Prudential 60 over World Cup, sadly we couldn't get in, so Hawkwind delivered us back to Buxton, in one piece but a little weary.

Hawkwind. With grateful thanks to Robyn.

When I first started playing senior cricket at Buxton the club had only just started playing league cricket. In those days the Sunday fixtures might be of a much higher standard than those of a Saturday. A number of the excellent players from the D&C and former local first-class professionals like A.B. (Brian) Jackson, Alan (Bud) Hill, or David Millner, as well as some others who played as pro's in the major leagues, would play on a Sunday. I think there was great kudos for some clubs to come and play on a county ground, and many of the 'wandering' or 'grasshopper' teams, who had no fixed abode of their own, would often make up the fixture list. I particularly remember a team called Craven Gentlemen, who were regular visitors and that one of their team drove a Rolls Royce, not a common sight in cricket club car parks.

Searching through my father's papers I found evidence of a cricket league as such, going back to 1956. It may have gone back further but I have no evidence - or when it ended.

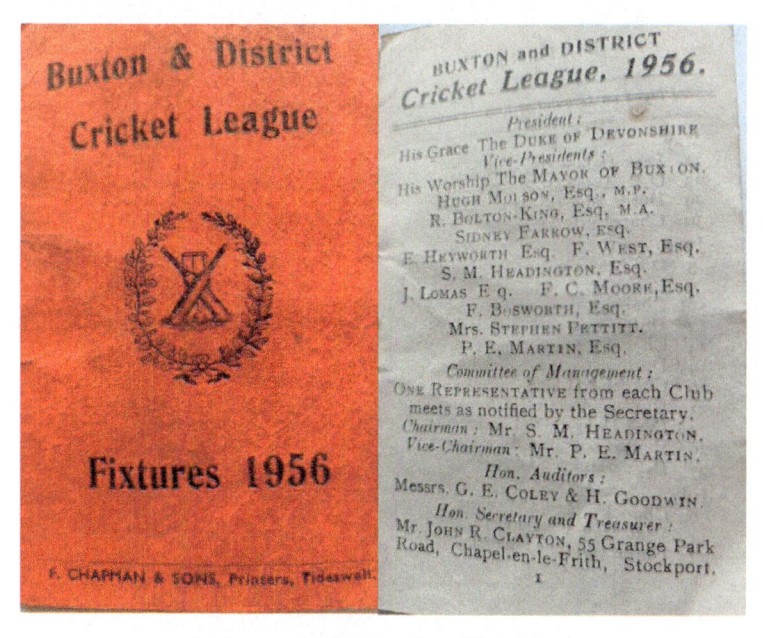

Buxton & District Cricket League

Fixtures 1956

F. CHAPMAN & SONS, Printers, Tideswell.

BUXTON and DISTRICT Cricket League, 1956.

President:
His Grace The DUKE OF DEVONSHIRE
Vice-Presidents:
His Worship The MAYOR OF BUXTON.
HUGH MOLSON, Esq., M.P.
R. BOLTON-KING, Esq., M.A.
SIDNEY FARROW, Esq.
E. HEYWORTH Esq.   F. WEST, Esq.
S. M. HEADINGTON, Esq.
J. LOMAS Esq.   F. C. MOORE, Esq.
F. BOSWORTH, Esq.
Mrs. STEPHEN PETTITT.
P. E. MARTIN, Esq.

Committee of Management:
ONE REPRESENTATIVE from each Club meets as notified by the Secretary.
Chairman: Mr. S. M. HEADINGTON.
Vice-Chairman: Mr. P. E. MARTIN.

Hon. Auditors:
Messrs. G. E. COLEY & H. GOODWIN.
Hon. Secretary and Treasurer:
Mr. JOHN R. CLAYTON, 55 Grange Park Road, Chapel-en-le-Frith, Stockport.

Some notable local residents here.

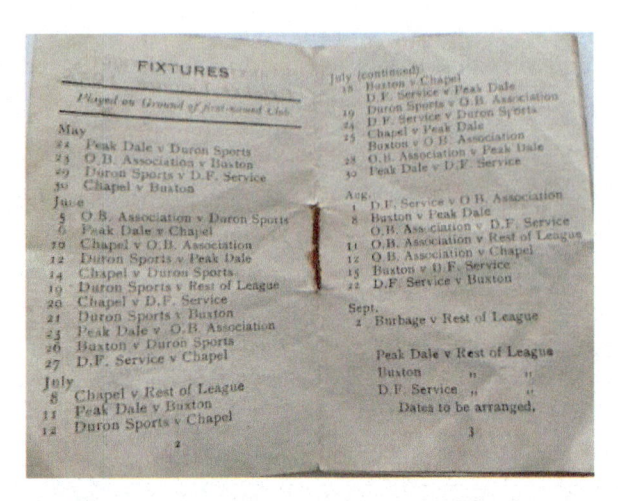

Interesting that everybody played a Rest of the League team, I assume to add fixtures.

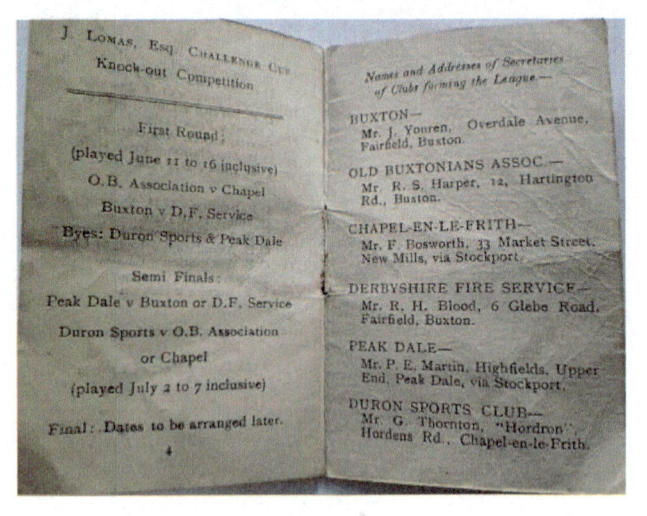

The dates for the above fixtures show that it was a mid-week league with only six teams, Buxton and Chapel being the two recognised clubs. I'm guessing the other teams were assembled specifically for this competition, but I might be wrong. I don't recall Peak Dale ever having a regular team, this is my only knowledge of a Buxton College Old Boys XI or a Derbyshire Fire Service XI. I worked at Duron Brake Linings for many years and was told that before my time they used to have a number of games, but I only recall one fixture, against our biggest customer, Godfrey Holmes Ltd over in Lincoln.

Also, in my father's papers I found a copy of the Buxton Cricket Club Membership Book for 1953, the clubs Centenary. (I was yet but a twinkle!)

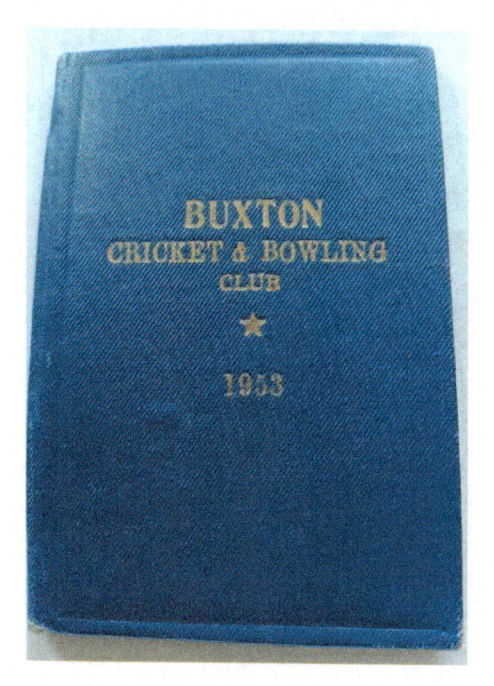

An elegant cover.

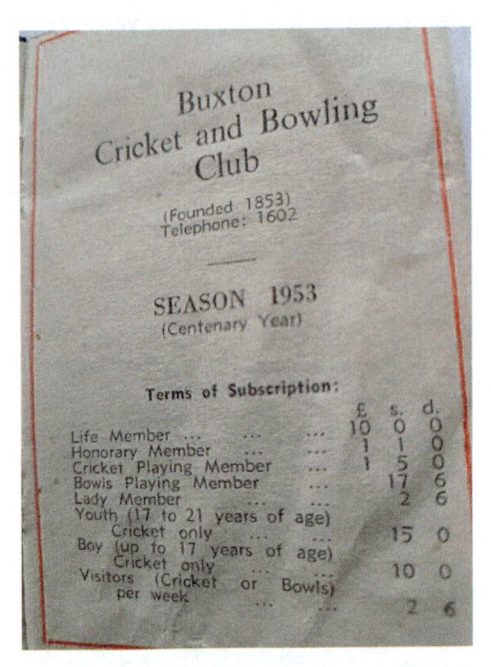

The playing member subscription equates to about £39 now.

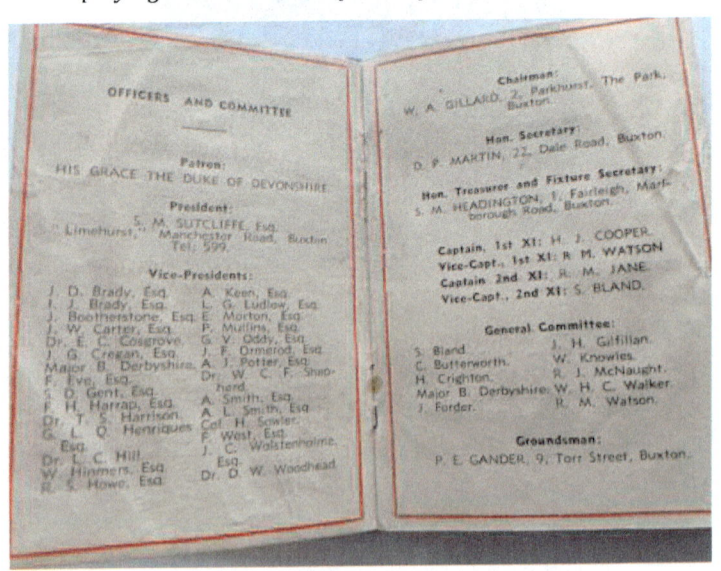

My dad on the general committee.

FIXTURES FIRST ELEVEN
SATURDAY

Date	Opponents	G'nd
April 25	Withington	H
May 2	Bowdon	A
9	Old Edwardians	H
16	Burton-on-Trent	H
23	Darley Dale	A
25 (Mon.)	Old West Bridgfordians	H
27 (Weds.)		
29 (Fri.)	Newton Heath	H
30 (Sat.)	Maxonians	H
June 6	Sheffield Collegiate	A
13	Bramhall	H
20	Burton-on-Trent	A
27	Heaton Mersey	A
July 4	Alderley Edge	H
11	York Wanderers	H
18		
25		
29 (Wed.)	M.C.C. (11-30)	H
Aug. 1	Bramhall	A
3 (Mon.)	Heaton Mersey	H
8	Darley Dale	H
15	Sheffield Collegiate	H
22	County Match	
29	Alderley Edge	A
Sept. 5	Bowdon	H
12		

Maxonian - a native of Macclesfield.

SUNDAY FIXTURES

Date	Opponents	G'nd
April 26	Sheffield University	H
May 3		
10	Sheffield Collegiate	H
17	Denstone College	H
24	East Levenshulme	H
31	Little Stoke	H
June 7	Oakham	H
14	Mansfield Colliery	H
21	The Cestrians	H
28	Manchester C.I.D.	H
July 5	Sheffield Cutlers	H
12	York Wanderers	H
19	Bootle	H
* 26	The Crusaders	H
Aug. 2	Whalley Range	H
9	Old Xaverians	H
16	Longsight	H
23		
30	Adwick-on-Dearne	H
Sept. 6	Stockport	H
13	Weaste	H

Cestrians - from Chester. Old Xaverians - from Liverpool.

39

FIXTURES SECOND ELEVEN
SATURDAY

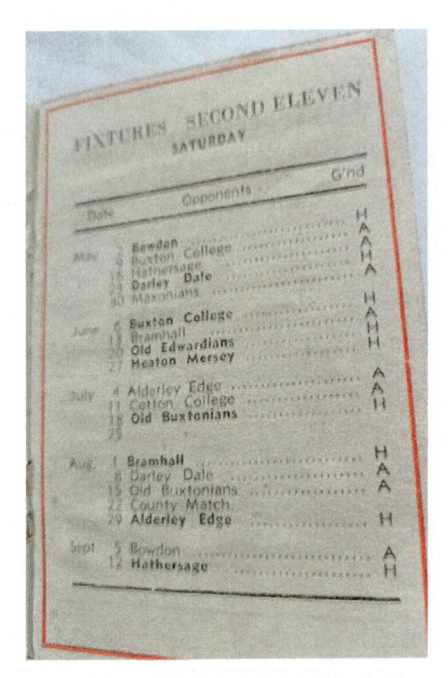

Date	Opponents	G'nd
May 2	Bowden	H
9	Buxton College	A
16	Hathersage	A
23	Darley Dale	H
30	Maxonians	A
June 6	Buxton College	H
13	Bramhall	A
20	Old Edwardians	H
27	Heaton Mersey	H
July 4	Alderley Edge	A
11	Cotton College	A
18	Old Buxtonians	H
25		
Aug. 1	Bramhall	H
8	Darley Dale	A
15	Old Buxtonians	A
22	County Match	
29	Alderley Edge	H
Sept. 5	Bowdon	A
12	Hathersage	H

Old Edwardians - O B's of King Edward VII School Sheffield.

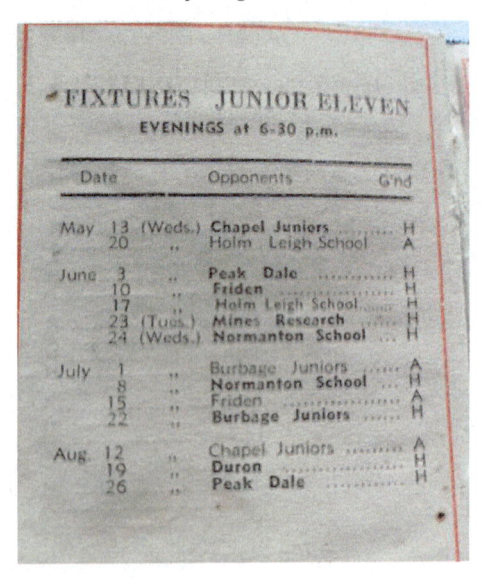

FIXTURES JUNIOR ELEVEN
EVENINGS at 6-30 p.m.

Date		Opponents	G'nd
May 13	(Weds.)	Chapel Juniors	H
20	,,	Holm Leigh School	A
June 3	,,	Peak Dale	H
10	,,	Friden	H
17	,,	Holm Leigh School	H
23	(Tues.)	Mines Research	H
24	(Weds.)	Normanton School	H
July 1	,,	Burbage Juniors	A
8	,,	Normanton School	A
15	,,	Friden	A
22	,,	Burbage Juniors	H
Aug. 12	,,	Chapel Juniors	A
19	,,	Duron	H
26	,,	Peak Dale	H

Holm Leigh School was a Prep school and had a number of premises in the Corbar area of town.

In 1905 the Brittain family moved to Buxton so Vera Brittain (later the mother of the politician Shirley Williams) and her brother Edward could attend Prep School. Edward did attend Holm Leigh before moving on to Uppingham School.

Edward, as with so many of his contempories perished on the battlefields of WW1. There is a memorial plaque in St John's Church commemorating 25 such alumni.

In 1959 the school moved to Sandbach in Cheshire and later the schools Junior house became the John Duncan school.

In my early teens I would start making up the numbers for the second team, and would be a regular member of the mid-week eleven. There were never a lot of mid-week fixtures, perhaps half a dozen or so across the summer. The glamour of these fixtures was never in doubt with games against the likes of Burbage CC, a local area of Buxton that somehow managed to run its own cricket team, they had a small ground just off Green Lane, (see cover) now used as the second ground of Buxton C.C. Friden Brick Works was situated 10 miles outside of Buxton at Newhaven on the Ashbourne Road. In those days it did exactly what it says on the tin, but these days I understand it is a far more technical and sophisticated company manufacturing and processing 'Refractory Minerals' (whatever those are?). Chelmorton is a village just four or five miles outside of Buxton just off the same Ashbourne Road. I recall playing in a fixture at Chelmorton when in the scorebook I read that in a previous Chelmorton match, the entire home team was made up by the same family. Three or four brothers, farmers I think, and their offspring. The team sheet read, Boam, Boam, Boam, Boam, Boam, Boam, Boam, Boam, Boam and Boam. One of whom, Stephen, I was at school with.

The makeup of the mid-week eleven was a veritable mish-mash, a pot pourri, indeed a salmagundi of styles, ages and physiques.

These would include those club members who had reached a certain age, all cane pads and spiked batting gloves, who at the very most might jog/walk a single. They would field at slip but couldn't bend and would call for the junior, fielding at third man, to run in and field the ball from gully.

The height of fashion back in the day.

There might be a couple of half-handy cricketers who just couldn't play at weekend, but the team would always be made up with a few juniors, because, somebody had to fetch the ball.

The Midweek eleven of my early years was once quite accurately described as 'a fine blend of youth and incompetence.'

WHEN SATURDAY COMES

A couple of fixtures spring to mind. From my very earliest days of scoring/playing, late sixties. Even if selected to play I would always be the scorer as well, someone else taking over if I was needed to bat, I was never gone long...

After the match my first duty would be to copy into our book, the opposition's innings - from their score-book - unless some kindly soul had done it for us.

One match that sticks vividly in my mind was a fixture against Chatsworth away. It was one of those blisteringly hot days that were all too rare. For some reason I don't remember scoring, perhaps I'd been given a couple of overs' respite to stretch my legs. I recall a boundary perambulation, a common practice amongst all cricketers, with my brother Chas. 'Our kid' was a fairly good ornithologist, and as we walked alongside the slow flowing, babbling Derwent River, the magnificent Chatsworth House as a backdrop, he suddenly stopped and pointed out a kingfisher, perched on a fence post some yards ahead. We stood statue still, just watching the beautiful bird. Alas, it didn't dive into the water and exit with a stickleback in its mouth, it just flew off seeking a more fruitful stretch of river.

One other thing I remember about that day was that Chatsworth had a fearful fast opening bowler whose name was Wragg. I didn't have to face him, and definitely remember being glad I didn't have to.

Cricket at Chatsworth. Picture courtesy of Chatsworth Cricket Club.

At about the same time as this, the second eleven had a fixture at Ashley, a pretty little village ground near Altrincham. Cars were parked outside the ground on a wide grass verge. There would be fewer cars in those days - not everybody had one - but our captain Brian, had a lovely late 50's/early 60's sports car, it was cream coloured and this being another lovely day had the soft top folded back. (I'm hopeless on cars, but it may have been a Midget?)

The day passed peacefully, of the match I remember nothing, much more memorable though was the furore afterward when captain Brian discovered that the cows in the field next to where he had parked, had spent the afternoon leaning over the hedge and snacking on his convertible's hood, which, when put up, looked like Swiss cheese.

It's curious when looking back on my earliest playing/scoring memories just what sticks and has remained and just how much you don't recall at all. I also wonder just how accurate my memories are, and if contemporaries would remember given incidents differently.

Another incident that has etched its existence into my memory file happened at Elvaston near Derby, or did it, because close to Elvaston is Alvaston, it was definitely one of these. What I can say for certain is that it was the ground that in the late 60's to whenever, used a converted railway carriage as the dressing rooms and pavilion.

The incident in question was a catch, a caught and bowled, and was executed by one Jim Donnelly. Jim (Mr. Donnelly to me) was the Deputy Headmaster at the local Catholic school, Thomas More. He had represented Yorkshire at U18 level before the war. He was a short and stocky bald-headed man who at this stage of his cricketing career it would be fair to say, was not perhaps as mobile as he once was. That sentiment however was rubbished on this particular day, as the batsman leathered a straight drive back to within a few feet of where he was in his follow through, like Clark Kent, Mr Donnelly took off on a horizontal plane and clutched the crimson traveller one handed, before coming down to earth with a still firm grip on the ball. His own team-mates and players in the opposition alike, all stood open-mouthed before much celebratory back slapping ensued.

BUXTON CRICKET CLUB'S FIRST ELEVEN

ck-end's picture of Buxton's 1st XI. On the front row are (left to right) K. M. Roberts, G. K. Johnston, W. E. Knowles, G. Carter; back row: D. M , G. Moorhouse, D. Wilks, F. Mason, T. Harris, J. Donnelly.

The above photograph is from the Buxton Advertiser dated 18/05/1951. A young Jim Donnelly can be seen at the end of the back row and my father is seated No.4 on the front row. (Only 10 turned up for the photo!)

There is a scene in the film Lawrence of Arabia, where Lawrence clambers to the top of a huge dune, to be greeted by the sight of a massive ship sailing through the sand. It was of course sailing through the unseen Suez Canal.

I recall scoring at Oughtrington Park CC, (near Manchester) when exactly the same phenomenon greeting my unbelieving eyes, except this time of course the canal was the Manchester Ship Canal and the boats were sailing through fields of wheat. It was a quite awesome spectacle and the boats were surprisingly big.

PROPER CRICKET

Looking up the hill at Buxton.

It doesn't look like its uphill but by the time you've bowled 12-15 overs up it I can assure you it is! Picture courtesy of Mathew Poole.

To the best of my knowledge and apart from the local mid-week league as highlighted above, Buxton C.C. did not play league cricket.

So, I was surprised to read in the earliest online document, 1946, of the then named, Manchester and District Cricket Association that Buxton C.C. were an affiliate member but did not participate in the league structure.

In fact, there were 33 members but only 21 played 'league' fixtures.

The next online record is 1949 and Buxton C.C.'s status is unchanged. However, in the next available record, 1951, Buxton C.C. are no longer members of the association.

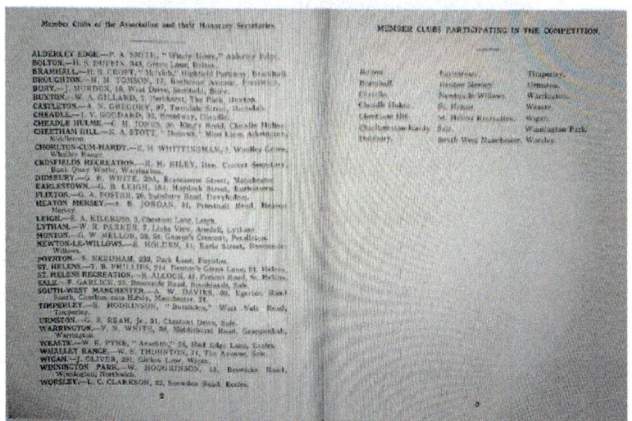

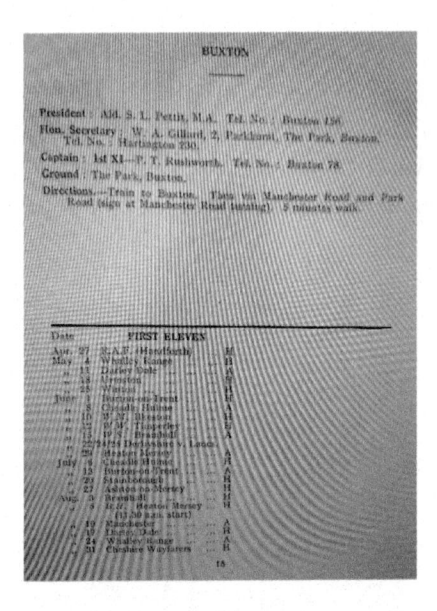

As a young boy I remember Bill Gillard, he drove a most beautiful burgundy red Alvis motor car.

After a few years of existing as a non-league cricket club, in 1969 Buxton CC decided it was time for a change and they were accepted into the Manchester Association Cricket League. The local Derbyshire and Cheshire Cricket League had been going since 1952.

This meant a whole new experience for everybody involved, suddenly we were going to exotic places like Weaste. (Oughtrington Park mentioned above was probably another early fixture.)

Weaste (Now Monton & Weaste CC) was a place I'd never heard of. On first arriving at the ground, you couldn't help but notice that the boundary on one side of the ground was formed by the back of a large stand overlooking and belonging to Salford Rugby League Club. I felt sure that Coronation Street was just around the corner.

Weaste CC actually forms one of my earliest memories of playing for Buxton 2's. In a league fixture I was number 11 and went to the wicket with Buxton needing 3 to win. I was told to block it and leave the heroics to the bloke at the other end. But, I ask you, who can block a half volley outside the off stump. Foot down and thump, straight back over the bowler's head for four and victory. I remember this incident so well because it happened so infrequently during my playing days.

There has been very little unpleasantness on the playing field during my time as player or official. One of the more unsavoury incidents took place on a chilly day in west Manchester.

Playing for Buxton 2's I was bowling and had the opposition batsman caught low down in the gully. The batsman was happy that the catch was good, we were all delighted and congratulating each other when I noticed the umpire at my end, who was the opposition captain, looking at the ground and deliberately shaking his head from side to side, the batsman also noticed this and quickly remade his ground. 'How was that', I bellowed, echoed by our captain approaching from the slips, the gully fielder still holding the ball high, 'Not Out', said their captain, still not looking anyone in the eye. If this was league cricket, you could stick it where the sun don't shine. Steam was coming out of my ears, I was only subdued by the arrival of our captain, a very canny Yorkshireman by the name of Irving Gawthorpe, who put his arm around my shoulder, told me not to worry about it, and whispered 'You're just going to have to bowl him'. What a great story this would be if in my next over I took his middle peg out, sadly not to be, Irving in fact took me off and dispatched me to the boundary to cool off a little more.

In what was not such a canny move, I was fielding on the boundary in front of the Pavilion when a couple of overs later, said batsman was out. Of course, he had to walk past me to get to the Pavilion, 'I thought you batted better in your second innings' I offered, at which point he approached me with a raised bat, I stood my ground, said something along the lines of C.U. Next Tuesday, and off he walked.

Faith in human nature was slightly restored when after the game in a decidedly chilly bar area, said batsman approached me and Irving, this after their captain had had to 'leave early'. He apologised for not walking, told us what the whole dressing room thought of the captain and said that he didn't think he would be by next week. We learned not long after that the captain had moved to another club.

Fortunately, such incidents were very few and far between, in fact other than a little disrespect when I was umpiring many years later nothing of an unsavoury nature comes to mind.

Buxton C.C. stayed in the Manchester Association with varying degrees of success for the next ten years or so.

Looking back through the records of the Association a number of stalwart members of the club made the annual averages, both batting and bowling, some a number of times.

The qualification to make the batting averages was an average of 25 from at least 10 innings. The bowling qualification was 25 wickets at an average of 18 or under.

In the club's first season, two bowlers made the grade, my brother Cec and Geoff Howe.

In the following season my brother Cec again made the grade, this time with Irving Gawthorpe and in the Second team averages, Duncan Jackson appeared in both the batting and bowling.

In 1971 the club registered no players reaching the required level.

However, 1972 was a much better year, Alan (Bud) Hill, in only ten games managed to average 47.22, in August of 1972 Bud made his first-class debut for Derbyshire and went on to amass 12356 runs with 18 centuries and 65 fifties. In the same season, Martin Drabble, a very hasty bowler, took 36 wickets at only 9.31 apiece. In the second team that season, Sergit (Gerry) Singh took 28 wickets at only 6.07 apiece, with the ever reliable and consistent John Barber taking 29 wickets at 14.62 apiece.

In 1973 my brother Cec took 49 league wickets at 17.47 and in all cricket for Buxton that summer took all but 100 wickets.

Some of the other excellent club cricketers who made the lists were: Nigel Forrest, Bill Torrance, Peter Cockram, A.B.Jackson, Nick

Smith, Martin Jackson (Duncan's son), Hugh Rogers, Arthur Grattan and in 1977 a fresh faced whipper-snapper that is yours truly finished the season having bowled 270.5 overs, 72 maidens, 653 runs and 46 wickets at 14.2 apiece.

I would give special mention to Hugh Rogers who in the above season took 36 wickets at 6.94 each. Hugh performed to those kinds of numbers for five or so seasons, very consistent indeed. He worked for the Halifax Building Society and I think left the area with a promotion, but he was a formidable bowler at that level.

There are two other cricketers that need a mention when I look back at these times.

The first is David Millner. My dad used to say to me, 'Boy (Its what he called me) if you want to learn how to bat properly, watch David.'

Dad would always tell you if asked, that David was the best 17/18-year-old batsman he'd ever seen.

David went on to play 31 first class games for Derbyshire in the early 60's with a top score of 80 against Kent at Derby in 1961. I was lucky to take the field with David in my early years, but I vividly remember 'scoring' a lot of his runs from that little box perched above the pavilion doors.

FIRST TEAMS, FIRST DIVISION — BATTING
Qualification — 10 Innings, Average 25.00

NAME	Inns.	N.O.	Highest Score	Runs	Av.
N. A. Bradshaw (Wigan)	19	6	81*	663	51.00
D. A. Peet (Wigan)	16	7	78*	457	50.78
D. Ainsworth (Bolton)	21	3	109*	836	46.49
R. K. Brookes (Monton)	19	2	111*	678	39.88
D. J. Walker (Worsley)	18	1	161	651	38.29
D. J. Milner (Buxton)	20	6	78	532	38.00
J. Walsh (Didsbury)	15	4	80*	415	37.73
N. Fairbrother (Grappenhall)	20	7	95*	479	36.85
K. Livesley (Weaste)	13	8	46*	180	36.00
N. Sharp (Grappenhall)	23	4	86*	681	35.84
A. Hayhurst (Worsley)	17	2	86*	518	34.53
A. Stevens (Whalley Range)	19	4	86*	493	32.87
B. Sproates (Flixton)	15	1	110*	451	32.21
D. Herd (Timperley)	20	3	100*	533	31.35
K. Northey (St. Helens)	18	4	81*	426	30.43

Manchester Association 1980 Batting Averages

FIRST TEAMS, FIRST SECTION — BATTING
Qualification — 10 Innings, Average 25.00

NAME	Inns.	N.O.	Highest Score	Runs	Av.
N. Smith (Buxton)	20	1	103	688	36.21
G. J. Cropper (St. Helens)	17	6	100*	394	35.82
D. J. Walker (Worsley)	20	4	80	543	33.94
D. Herd (Timperley)	18	0	76	595	33.00
K. Northey (St. Helens)	16	6	69*	326	32.60
P. Thompson (Lytham)	12	3	69	265	29.44
H. Morris (Grappenhall)	17	1	105*	451	28.18
C. J. Curtis (Worsley)	17	7	74*	281	28.10
C. J. Hall (Worsley)	20	4	59*	448	28.00
N. Wood (Timperley)	14	3	42	293	26.64
S. Baloch (Lytham)	13	1	68	316	26.33
B. Milner (Buxton)	20	0	67	522	26.10
D. Crompton (Bolton)	18	4	50	362	25.85
I. Collins (Didsbury)	15	2	—	326	25.08

Manchester Association 1979 Batting Averages

The second player that deserves a special mention is on the list above and that's Nick Smith. Dad would say that after David Millner, Nick was the best 17/18 years old batsman he'd ever seen.

Nick was an exceptional opening batsman who consistently scored runs, took wickets - off spin- and fielded better than anyone else. Very quick in mind and body and probably the player that practiced more than anyone else I ever played with.

Nick, like so many others, was tragically taken much too young in October 2020.

Our last season in the Manchester Association was 1980 when Buxton finished a very creditable second to the league champions Grappenhall. For whom, the records show, a 15 years old young man by the name of Neil Fairbrother finished 9th in the league batting averages with a not bad return of 36.85

The aforementioned David Millner was 6th.

The Membership Book and Fixture List for our final season in the Manchester Association.

**BUXTON
CRICKET, BOWLING
and
LAWN TENNIS
CLUB**

(Founded 1853)

★

SEASON 1980

★

(Telephone Buxton 2602)

OFFICERS AND COMMITTEE

Patron:
HIS GRACE THE DUKE OF DEVONSHIRE, M.C.

Hon. Life Members:
P. Gander, Esq.
K. R. Jones, Esq.

President:
W. E. Knowles, Esq.

Vice-Presidents:

J. Bootherstone, Esq.
I. J. Brady, Esq.
T. Catterick, Esq.
J. Donnelly, Esq.
J. B. Ellis, Esq.
H. Holland, Esq.
A. B. Jackson, Esq.
R. M. Jane, Esq.
R. McNaught, Esq.

G. Lomas, Esq.
D. P. Martin, Esq.
R. D. Millican, Esq.
F. C. Moore, Esq.
J. W. P. Quayle, Esq.
R. Stafford, Esq.
B. Stocks, Esq.
R. M. Watson, Esq.
F. C. Allen, Esq.

CRICKET SECTION

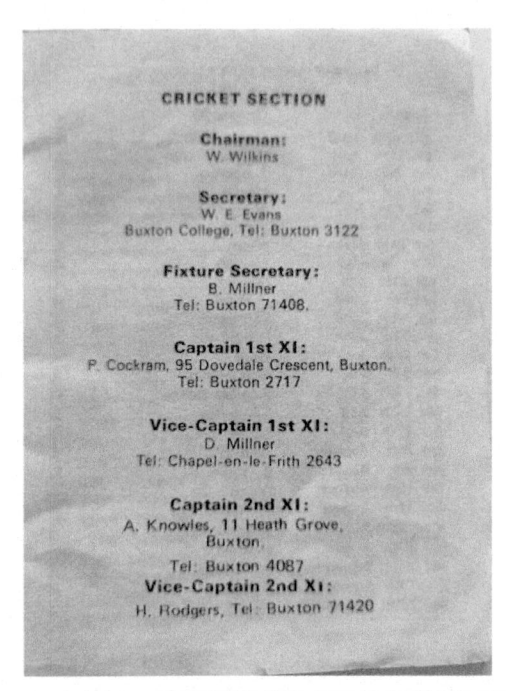

Chairman:
W. Wilkins

Secretary:
W. E. Evans
Buxton College, Tel: Buxton 3122

Fixture Secretary:
B. Millner
Tel: Buxton 71408.

Captain 1st XI:
P. Cockram, 95 Dovedale Crescent, Buxton.
Tel: Buxton 2717

Vice-Captain 1st XI:
D. Millner
Tel: Chapel-en-le-Frith 2643

Captain 2nd XI:
A. Knowles, 11 Heath Grove, Buxton.
Tel: Buxton 4087

Vice-Captain 2nd XI:
H. Rodgers, Tel: Buxton 71420

1980 FIXTURES FOR BUXTON C.C. — 1st XI DIVISION 1

Date	Opponents	G'nd
Sat 12th April	Grappenhall	H
Sat 19th April	Whalley Range	A
Sat 26th April	Timperley	H
Sat 3rd May	Weaste	A
Sat 10th May	Winton	H
Sat 17th May	Bolton	A
Sat 24th May	Wigan	H
Mon 26th May	Flixton	A
Sat 31st May	Monton	A
Sat 7th June	Lytham	H
Sat 14th June	St. Helens	H
Sat 21st June	Didsbury	A
Sat 28th June	Worsley	H
Sat 5th July	Grappenhall	A
Sat 12th July	Whalley Range	H
Sat 19th July	Timperley	A
Sat 26th July	Weaste	H
Sat 2nd August	Winton	A
Sat 9th August	Bolton	H
Sat 16th August	Wigan	A
Sat 23rd August	Flixton	H
Mon 25th August	Monton	H
Sat 30th August	Lytham	A
Sat 6th September	St. Helens	A
Sat 13th September	Didsbury	H
Sat 20th September	Worsley	A

1980 FIXTURES FOR BUXTON C.C. — 2nd XI DIVISION 1

Date	Opponents	G'nd
Sat 12th April	Grappenhall	A
Sat 19th April	Prescot	H
Sat 26th April	Timperley	A
Sat 3rd May	Weaste	H
Sat 10th May	Winton	A
Sat 17th May	Bolton	H
Sat 24th May	Wigan	A
Mon 26th May	Flixton	H
Sat 31st May	Urmston	H
Sat 7th June	Lytham	A
Sat 14th June	St. Helens	A
Sat 21st June	Didsbury	H
Sat 28th June	Worsley	A
Sat 5th July	Grappenhall	H
Sat 12th July	Prescot	A
Sat 19th July	Timperley	H
Sat 26th July	Weaste	A
Sat 2nd August	Winton	H
Sat 9th August	Bolton	A
Sat 16th August	Wigan	H
Sat 23rd August	Flixton	A
Mon 25th August	Urmston	A
Sat 30th August	Lytham	H
Sat 6th September	St. Helens	H
Sat 13th September	Didsbury	A
Sat 20th September	Worsley	H

All Manchester Association Games commence at 2.00 p.m. prompt.

After its spell in the Manchester Association, the club joined the North Staffs and South Cheshire Cricket League.

Snow joke! ● Buxton Cricket Club 2nd XI captain Andrew Knowles inspects the snow-covered Park wicket on Saturday morning with prospects bleak for their home game against Barlaston. The weather later relented to allow the visitors to score 125-3 before play was finally abandoned for the day.

Not the first time we've had Snow in Buxton. Can you believe we actually played later the same day? 'Eeee we were tough oop north.' Picture from the Buxton Advertiser courtesy Geoff Needham.

This was a different animal altogether, longer games and what's more, many of the teams had paid professionals.

When I say paid professionals, these weren't just players who were a tad better than average.

The records of the NS&SC still show that the second-best season's return for wickets was 97 by Garfield St. Aubrun Sobers in 1964. The best return for runs in a season was by Kim Barnett, 1,408 in 2004. The fastest century took only 50 balls and was scored by one Shahid Afridi, Boom Boom.

Many other famous names have graced the league, Wes Hall and Roy Gilchrist played at Great Chell whose ground, which no longer exists, was known as the Lords of the Potteries. Just down the road was Norton CC whose teams have been graced by not only the aforementioned Gary Sobers but Frank Worrall and Jim Laker as well.

Although I haven't been involved with the NS&SC since the late 80's, I note that there have been a number of changes, some clubs, like

Great Chell no longer exist, other clubs have merged to ensure the future of cricket in what has always been a real hotbed of the game.

I was the captain of Buxton 2nds by the time we joined the NS&SC, and it was certainly an interesting first fixture, as The Park was covered in about 12-18 inches of snow. (not the picture shown). I spoke with the league secretary who was adamant, 'League Rules' said no fixture can be called off by the home team before the arrival of the Umpires. 'But they might not even be able to get into Buxton' I argued, 'Rules is rules', came the reply. In the end common sense did win out and so without ever playing a game in the competition Buxton C.C. had managed to achieve a first.

The playing regulations of the league were like none any of us had ever encountered. 110 overs was the maximum length of a match, so if you put the opposition in, you either had to bowl them out or wait till they declared. If you won the toss and batted first it was awkward to bat, say 60 overs, only giving the opposition 50, but if in doing so you lost quick wickets it might be necessary to bat well over half way.

There was the usual bonus point structure, a point for every two wickets taken, then when batting a point for reaching 100 and every subsequent 25 runs up to 200 as a max. These bonus points however, could only be won in the first 55 overs of an innings.

It was a good league and the playing regulations, though not universally loved, made it much more interesting and thought provoking to be the captain.

I scored my first league 50 at Barlaston, a knock remembered by me alone and, on one very hot August day, bowled 33 overs on the trot at Crewe Rolls Royce. My good friends Peter Hardman and Guy Rogers shared the same number of overs at the other end. Even off a much-shortened run 33 overs on the bounce is a pretty Herculean effort, if I say so myself. (I wish I'd weighed myself before and after I could have been one of those 'then and now' pictures for the slimming magazines!) We just couldn't get them out, and they just couldn't get enough runs. It was the holiday season, I had a couple of friends playing who weren't cricketers, and we just didn't have anyone else to bowl. Of course, we only had to bat 44 overs so an honourable draw resulted.

It would be at about this time a new member came to the club, he was English but had been living in North America, he moved to Buxton having taken a job with a local chemical company. He was tall and gangly but, bowled left arm over (always an asset, well nearly....) and, he said, quickly! So, his first game for us was at Betley, a pretty little ground about halfway between Newcastle under Lyme and Nantwich, and I gave him the first over. He did bowl quite quickly but unfortunately at fine leg, after the first three went for four byes, and having put a second fine leg in place, I reminded him that we could have no more fielders behind the wicket on leg side. He assured me he would get it right.... but when. As he got the ball a little straighter the batsmen started hitting it for four. After two overs, 0-18 with nearly as many extras conceded, I took him off. He was incandescent, purple with rage, my captaincy was lamentable, I explained I was going to give him a go from the other end...in a while. Well, I did try him some overs later from the other end and would love to report that he skittled Betley out, but no, his second spell was hardly any better than his first, he finished with something like five overs, 0 for 38. With a few more extras to add. Those were his first and last five overs for the club. He resigned his membership and wrote to the committee describing and elaborating on my 'lamentable' captaincy. I must say, he was a much better writer than bowler.

My only brush with fame, (and it's a pretty hairless brush!) came one Saturday when for one reason or another I found myself in the first team playing against Norton CC at Buxton.

The professional for Norton was Dilip Doshi, who took 114 test wickets for India in 33 matches and had played a number of seasons at Warwickshire. We had done reasonably well and had a goodish score on the board when I strode to the wicket, number 9 or 10 and took guard against Dilip. The first ball he sent down was a long-hop outside leg, I stepped across and smote it for four runs to the leg side, a good distance as we were playing on the edge of the square near the tennis courts, Dilip was bowling from the Pavilion end and Buxton has a large playing area. Sadly, the playing area was too large as Dilip bowled me the same delivery again, this time I hit it skywards, straight into the hands of a fielder who wasn't there the ball before. As I walked back to the Pavilion and past Dilip, he gave me a most charming smile. So, I troubled the scorers to the tune of 4W.

One of the most beautiful cricket grounds in the country. Buxton CC. Picture: Colin Budenburg - Precision Pilot Drones.

Towards the end of the 1985 season, there are no online records so I can't tell who we had played or where, but after the game a number of the team, as per usual, were enjoying a post-match libation in the Bakers Arms which was on West Road. (*Now, sadly no longer, but there is a book to be written there, I'm sure.*)

I remember thinking that more players than usual had popped down for a pint that evening, when in through the door walked a Nun, carrying a collection box. She stopped to speak to a couple of people then, when reaching my table put down her collection box and asked, 'Are you Andrew?', 'I am' says I, at which point, grabbing her habit, she ripped it apart... it was Velcro'd, to exhibit what I can only describe as extremely flimsy lingerie over quite a full figure. She worked her way around the table and sat on my knee, accompanied by much cheering from the other members of Buxton 2's, including, as I could see over her shoulder, some very exaggerated sexual mimicry from the late Tommy Howe. At this point, if this was one of *those* kinds of books, I should report that she stood me up, threw me across two tables and rode me into next Tuesday. What she did do was put her arm around my neck, give me a peck on the cheek and whispered Happy Birthday Andrew. She then stood up, not a moment too soon I hasten to add, re-velcro'd herself and left the pub.

This was my thirtieth birthday present from my wonderful teammates.

At this point I shall regale you with two my favourite cricketing anecdotes. The NS&SC Cricket League did have good annual dinners and speakers. One year the speaker was Frank 'Typhoon' Tyson. He was widely regarded as one of England's finest fast bowlers, to some, Tom Graveney for one, the quickest. He told the following story that I have loved re-telling ever since.

Frank started: (Put your best Aussie accent on to read...)

I was talking to Don Tallon (one of Australia's finest test wicket-keepers) *one day when he said to me, 'Did you hear the story about when our Bill got the Don* (Bradman) *out'?* (Bill Tallon, Don's brother, played a few games for Queensland.) *'Well,' he continued, it was like this. 'We were playing South Australia in Brisbane and the pitch looked like there might just be a bit in it for our Bill. So, the South Australia openers come out, and before long one of them nicks off and I take the catch diving to my right and South Australia are 9-1. Out to the wicket strides The Don. A few overs later, our Bill's still bowling and the other opener nicks off, this time a straightforward catch to me, so there we have South Australia 32-2. Sometime later our Bill is bowling again, this time at Bradman who mis-times a drive and he's caught at point.*

South Australia 438-3.

I love that story.

In his superb book Engel's England, the journalist and cricket writer Matthew Engel recalls how traditionally the summer cricket tourists to England would play their first match at Worcester. This was certainly always true of the Australians.

In the 1930's Don Bradman toured the U.K. three times and, on each occasion, scored a **double hundred** at Worcester. He came again in 1948 but failed - out for **107**.

OXFORD

Another part of my cricketing life story that cannot go unrecorded would be that of the Oxford Tour.

For over 60 years now Buxton CC, or more accurately when on tour, the Buxton Strugglers, have enjoyed an annual cricket tour to Oxford to play the colleges and on the odd occasion the 'Authentics', who were the University second eleven.

The makeup of the tour was never just Buxton cricketers, a number of players from the Derbyshire and Cheshire league would regularly join us as well as others from even further afield.

We would leave Buxton on Tuesday morning, (always the day after the Whitsuntide Bank Holiday) stopping en-route for a nice greasy spoon. It was on one of these first trips that I was introduced, by Alan Burgess, to the fine delicacy that is Clarty Beans*.

We would get into Oxford late morning, deposit our bags in the Welsh Pony, where we always stayed in my day (though I believe it's now a Nando's) and would head out for our first look around Oxford and, if we weren't playing that day, no doubt our first pint.

In those early years of my touring, our first game was always at Worcester College which was literally just over the road from the Welsh Pony. I remember as though it was yesterday my first visit to Worcester College. We were given lunch in the refectory, not the sort of thing I'd done much of before. The chatter and hum of the students and the clatter of crockery echoing off the high walls and great arched windows. I remember walking across a quad with very old, medieval? cottages down one side, and then my memory tells me through a wooden door set into a very thick stone wall and out into a beautiful grass and gardened area. This wooden door may as well have been through a wardrobe as a wall, for I was in Narnia. There was hammering and sawing as a temporary stage was being erected which must have made it difficult for the fifteen or so students who, each carrying a script, were reciting their parts in what was obviously going to be a student production of a Shakespeare play.

A sandy coloured gravel path took us through a small wooded area and onto a most splendidly manicured cricket ground. The cricket pavilion nestled in the corner to the left was absolutely right and quintessentially English.

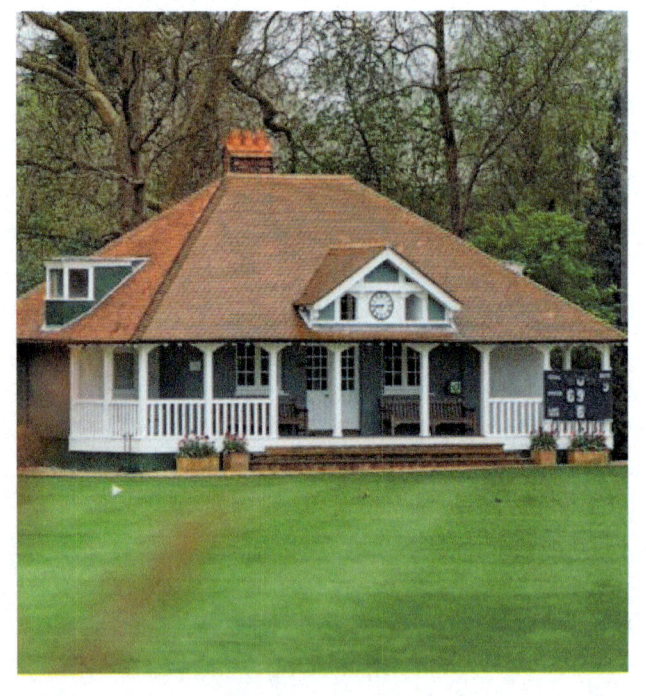

Worcester College CC. Picture courtesy of Worcester College.

It was at this most agreeable cricket ground that I encountered in the opposition two very fine rugby players. In the early 70's while studying medicine at Worcester, the England centre Charles Kent was in the opposition. Later, probably late-eighties none other than the winning captain of the first team to win the rugby World Cup,

New Zealand's David Kirk was in the opposing team.

Over the years, for one reason or another, we might find ourselves in Vincent's Club. 'Vinnie's' as I believe the regulars call it, is predominantly but not exclusively for those awarded a 'Blue' from Oxford. I have a somewhat hazy recollection of a game of Spoof being played with said David Kirk, in Vincent's, on the evening of the game at Worcester. I don't think I took part, I might have, but either way it's not the sort of thing that happens every day.

In those early years of my touring experience, the Wednesday game would always be against Brasenose College, at their equally impressive ground alongside the river Thames, or the Isis as it's known in Oxford, where we would play an all-day game, which allowed ample time to take advantage of the access to the river.

Brasenose College sports field - from the towpath.
Picture: Alamy photo stock.

A left turn on the towpath would bring you the short distance to Folly Bridge and the much-vaunted Oxford alehouse, The Head of the River, usually the first port of call for anyone not playing that particular day.

The touring party might be 14 or 15 strong and often players who couldn't make the full week would pop down for one or two days, so there was often scope for at least one day's rest!

A right turn out of the ground would take to you alongside the sports grounds of Queens College, immediately adjacent to that of Brasenose, and further on to the Donnington Bridge.

Before reaching the bridge however one would encounter the College Boathouses situated on the banks of the river. Our tour often coincided with 'Eights Week' which was the annual University Regatta. The riverside would be thronged with students cheering for their college, a gaudy display of brightly coloured blazers and straw boaters. From memory most of the boathouses were on the other side of the river, but there was at least one on our side.

Most of the boathouses would be flat-topped and so could be used as a viewing gallery and during 'Eights Week' as a bar as well.

It came to the attention of myself, Peter Hardman, perhaps a couple of others as we tentatively explored this opportunity that some of the colleges operated a traditional system of payment - or non-payment - for drinks, known as Battels. As I recall, you simply gave your name, and I think perhaps a fictitious room number/address? And you would be served with the drink *de jour* which was always Pimms.

I recall one afternoon where we seriously took advantage of this generous system, and have often wondered what the chances were that the college did have a student named John Smith, and if they did, how I hoped he would be a non-drinking divinity student. What fun they would have when he was presented with a bill for 7 or 8 large Pimms at the end of term.

The Thursday of the Oxford tour would often be the fixture with the Authentics, or Tics as they were universally known. Having no ground of their own, this fixture could be on any one of the many college grounds throughout the city. This was always great fun, travelling to a ground we might not have been to before. All the Oxford College grounds that I have been to, bar none, have been exceptional.

I have one main recollection of an Authentics game. I must say by the time Thursday arrives in Oxford the memory is getting a little hazy, and I'm adding 50 years onto that, but on the 30/05/1974 we had a game against the Tics played at New College, and in the opposition was a fast bowler by the name of Cantlay. The word on the street was that Imran Khan wouldn't pick him for the University first team because he was quicker than him, others thought that his action might have been questionable. Now I wouldn't know about that because I never faced Imran Khan, and I can't really tell you how quick Cantlay was either, because I never saw it. Never have I been more pleased to be bowled neck and crop first ball. I was almost back in the pavilion before Cantlay had finished his follow through, I remember praying that the umpire didn't shout no-ball. To say I didn't get behind it would be the understatement of the century.

I wasn't alone though, Mr. Cantlay removed a number of far better players than I ever was.

Of the three Knowles boys playing that day, we amassed between us thirteen runs. Big brother Cec, coming in at No.7, made a very respectable dozen, the second highest score in fact. Brother Charles batted last and was run-out for one, which, as I've already stated, left my fine knock.

On a personal note, (what do I mean? The whole book is a personal note...) though I have taken to the field with either of my brothers on many occasions, the instances are few and far between when all three of us took to the field together, this was one of those occasions.

The Three Amigos

Taken at Vincents Club Centenary Dinner ? 1987

The author, Chas and Cec Knowles.

The evidence of a none too successful day.

The 'Tics batted first.

A special mention should be given to the innings of Peter Cockram who, whilst all others were flailing around under the onslaught of Cantlay and Siviter, played a wonderfully composed innings of 43 n.o.

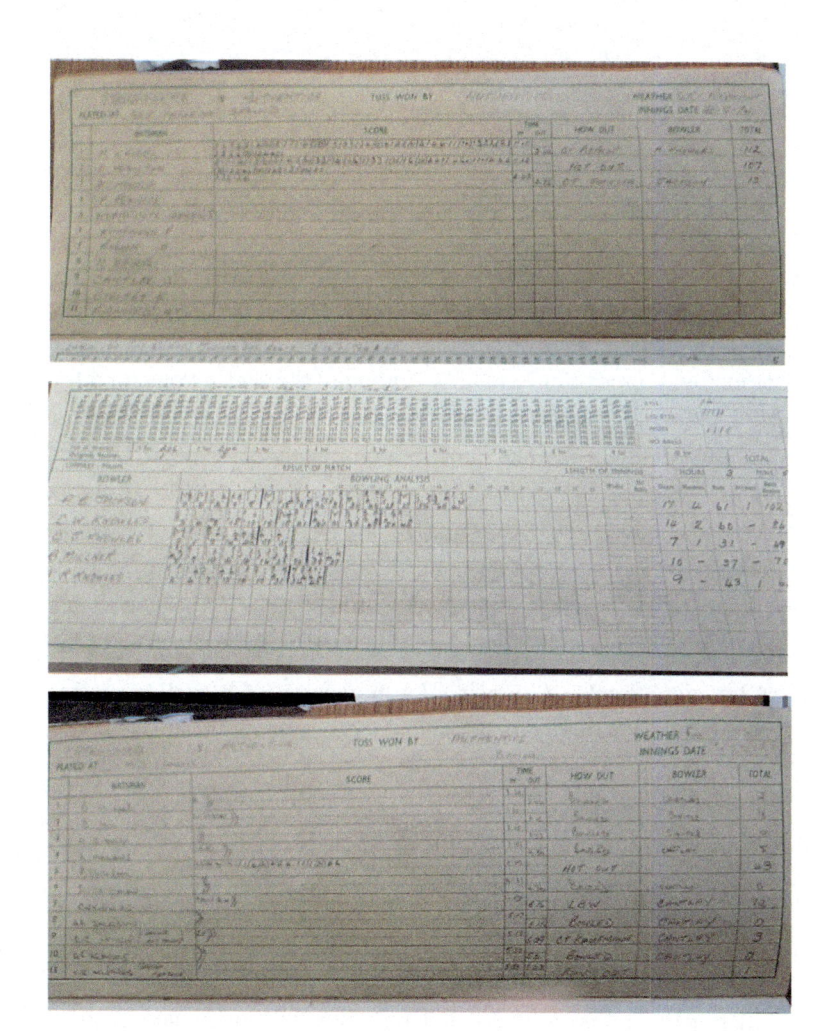

And Mr. Cantleys contribution.

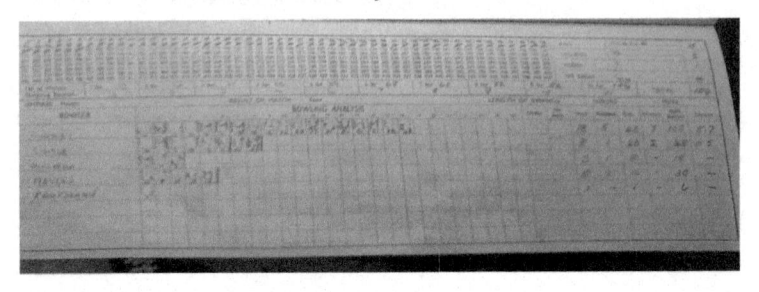

Thursday night of the tour, certainly in the early days was also the night we had a bit of a shindig. The teams played thus far, plus tomorrow's opposition, would be invited to the Welsh Pony for a few drinks. Few of course is a relative term, to some it's a measured amount, to others it's one short of completely blotto. On Thursday nights we would always, late on, be treated to the fine Welsh tenor voice of 'Snave', the Latin master at Buxton College. He would annually, climb onto a table and give a splendid rendition of the 'Engineers Wheel' with full body thrusting actions. (If at all possible, Bernard Hill would tie his shoelaces together while he was doing this.)

Imagine the Mr Chippsian Latin master of a well-respected grammar school, high on a table and in his splendid baritone Welsh voice, blasting out:

'An Engineer told me before he died,

That he knew a girl with a **** so wide.

(and that's quite enough of that, thanks, ed…)

Peter the landlord of the Welsh Pony might then give us one or both of his party pieces. He gave a splendid rendition of 'Down in the sewer shovelling up manure' and his favourite, 'Be I Berkshire be I buggery'.

Peter would grab people's attention and clap, perfectly in time with the rhythm of the piece:

> 'Down in the sewer, shovelling up manure,
> Watching all the t**** go flippity, flippity, flop....
> (and of that thank you. ed...)

> Then in a fine south of England rustic voice:
> 'Be I Berkshire, be I buggery,
> Oi comes up from Wareham,
> Where the girls wear Calico drawers,
> And the boys knows how to tear 'em.
> (Really? That is enough...)

I didn't know Peter very well, but he certainly had a good rapport with the more longstanding members of our touring party. He would stand at the hatch of the bar, the nearest optic to him an almost always nearly empty bottle of Stewart's Cream of the Barley Scotch Whisky, which he liked quite a lot. I remember arriving one Tuesday morning and entering the Pony with Alan Burgess, we found Peter in the bar by the hatch with a glass of something clear in his hand. Formal greeting over, Alan looked at Peter's glass, 'Gin' said Peter, almost spitting the word out, 'Doctor told me I had to give up whisky'.

Breakfasts were excellent at the Welsh Pony and before my first tour I was advised that not only were they mandatory, but you had to have a bottle of Guinness with your fry up each morning to wash it down... or up... which was more likely the result.

The only other rule I was told was, if you had been selected to play the next day you must be in bed by 6.00 in the morning.

I hasten to add here that I don't recall any of these rules being enforced.

The Friday fixture, after booking out of the Welsh Pony, was invariably against Christchurch College at their ground just off the

Iffley Road. They had wonderful sports facilities, immaculate tennis courts, a beautiful cricket square, and glorious clubhouse. Situated right next to the cricket ground was the athletics facility where in 1954 Sir Roger Bannister became the first person to run a sub four-minute mile.

I loved this cricket ground, so much so that after one particularly hairy Thursday night, I gave it my breakfast, just behind the sightscreen.

Our visits to Oxford were memorable for a number reasons, hence the re-wording of the old adage, 'What happens in Oxford, stays in Oxford'. However, there was one regular event that I am happy to recall in print. For a number of consecutive years, my good friend Peter 'Gaffer' Hardman and I would visit the Ashmolean Museum.

The purpose of this visit would be to go and view a superb painting by Rembrandt von Rijn. This painting, though very small, had fascinated us, simply by its sheer brilliance. It was kept, enclosed in a small case with a viewing glass front, possibly slightly magnified (if it was not by much), in a room full of other masterpieces, much larger and wall hanging. Nevertheless, it was this tiny painting of a head, no bigger than a paperback book, almost insignificant amongst its bigger and more illustrious companions, that had enthralled both Gaffer and myself from our very first viewing some tours earlier.

So here we were again on a bright and sunny, early June morning, taking the steps up to the great columned portico that was the grand entrance to the Ashmolean Museum. Once inside we knew where to go, after all we were visiting an old friend. Up the stairs, down a short corridor to a double-roomed gallery, a uniformed guard sat in the doorway, a position that enabled him to view both rooms.

We entered the room where the painting had always been, looked but it wasn't there, 'Perhaps it's in the other room' suggested Gaff. We walked through but there were no free-standing displays of any kind in either room, 'I'll ask the guard,' I said.

I caught the guards attention and approached him, 'Excuse me, don't know if you can help us or not, but there was always, in this room' indicating which one with a flick of hand, 'a case that stood about so high,' another handy indication, 'It had a painting of a head by Rembrandt in it, we visit it every year' this time I indicated Gaffer as though the guard might not have able to determine who the other half of we was! 'Do you know if it's been moved to another part of the museum?' I asked.

'I'm not sure sir' he replied, 'but if you give me a couple of minutes I'll try and find out for you'. With that he turned and walked to a shelf on the wall where he picked up a very old-fashioned black Bakelite telephone. Gaffer and I stood in the centre of the room admiring the paintings but always keeping half an eye on the guard.

The wonderful Ashmolean Museum. Picture: Alamy stock photo.

A couple of minutes later the guard replaced the receiver and made his way towards us. 'Gentlemen' he proceeded, 'the case is actually having a small repair done to it at this time, but if you go back down the stairs to the reception area, someone will meet you there', with that he did a half turn and indicated with his arm the doorway we should take to return downstairs. It was all terribly,

terribly British, even the very small salute he gave lifting his hand to his cap as we went on our way.

Once back down the stairs and having no idea what was about to happen next, we stood, gazing around in the reception area like two lost sheep. I looked at Gaff and he looked at me and we did a synchronized shoulder shrug, wondering how long we would be waiting there.

After less than a minute, from across the foyer, a huge oak door with burnished brass knob and push plate opened, and advancing towards us came a most dapper and well-groomed man, resplendent in a very smart suit and wearing a navy blue bow tie with white polka dots. Above this he had on the most serious looking pair of thick black rimmed glasses and a charming smile.

He looked from one to the other of us, 'Are you the gentlemen who would like to view the Rembrandt' he enquired, we nodded confirmation and he said 'Please follow me'.

He turned and we followed him back through the great door where, in front of us was the longest table either of us had ever seen, and completely covered in green baize. The table had on it lots of books of all shapes and sizes and many other unidentifiable, to us, objects.

Two fine high-backed chairs were at one end, leather padded with brass studs, which the gentleman pointed to and asked us to sit.

At this point he donned a pair of white cotton gloves and lifting quite the thickest book I have ever seen laid it on the table in front of us. He then turned to a row of the longest drawers you could imagine and soundlessly slid one open. Reaching in, he carefully lifted the small painting and turning, leaned it against the book he had just placed in front of us.

He looked down at the work of art and said, 'Gentlemen, you have exquisite taste, enjoy, but please don't touch' and with that he turned and busied himself with some other activity further along the table.

So, there we were, Gaffer Hardman and Andrew Knowles, sat in front of a small but beautiful, finely detailed painting of a man's head, by none other than Rembrandt. What its value was I couldn't guess, could Gaffer run fast enough entered my thoughts for only a split second. It was an unplanned and unexpected moment of real joy, that will live with me forever.

*

Peter 'Gaffer' Hardman

Picture courtesy of Robyn.

Peter 'Gaffer' Hardman was quite simply one of the nicest people I have ever known. Utterly altruistic, he would do anything for anyone. I understand, but am not surprised, that he was a much-loved teacher. A good cricketer, a very good footballer and a great friend. A proud family man but like too many such people he was taken too soon.

The world is a better place because Gaff was in it.

It is impossible for me to think of the Oxford tour without making a special mention of Alan Burgess and his invaluable contributions.

For many years, Alan was an outstanding member of Buxton Cricket Club. A fine wicket-keeper, an excellent batsman, and a shrewd 1st XI captain, he taught me a great deal.

Alan was also an exceptional curator of the cricket square. The fact that the pitches we played on were of county standard was almost entirely due to his diligence and passion for maintaining the sacred strip.

Beyond that, Alan took on the immense responsibility of organizing every aspect of the Oxford tour—arranging fixtures, securing accommodation, coordinating transport, and managing the tour party. He did this not only for every Oxford tour I attended but for many others as well.

A great deal of this book could not have been written without Alan's efforts, and for that, I extend my deepest thanks.

*Clarty beans - Two or three spoonfuls of baked beans popped into the frying pan with your sausage and bacon.

WARMINSTER

In October 1977 my brother Chas moved to the delightful Wiltshire town of Warminster, where he immediately joined the Cricket Club. Over the next few years I made many visits, always enjoying the old pavilion, George serving drinks behind the bar, meeting and making new friends.

Back Row, Scorer - (unknown), Andrew Pinnell, Colin Gilmour, John Baldwin, Chas Knowles, Eric Ludlow, Russell Stevens.

Front Row, Neil Stevens - not sure - Gerry Clarke and a young Doug Small.

Lingering in the background is Valentino Bartholomew, general help and my scorer when I captained the second team.

The little girl is Chas's daughter and my niece, Clare.

Picture courtesy Andrew Pinnell.

I would venture down for the annual club dinner, on one memorable occasion at the Old Bell Hotel the guest speaker was Hubert Doggart, who still holds the record for the highest score made by a debutant in English first class cricket, 215 against Lancashire in his first game for Cambridge University in 1948. He may even have been President of the MCC at the time, a post he held in the early 80's. Until 1985 he was the headmaster of The Kings School, Bruton.

I loved my visits to Warminster and I loved the club which clearly had some excellent young cricketers just making their way into the senior sides. So, when a business opportunity arose for me 1989 in Calne, just up the road, what better place to move to than somewhere I was already very fond of. What's more, my brother Chas who had long been a stalwart of the cricket club, was also moving on to pastures new, becoming a pub landlord up in Gloucestershire, we passed like ships in the night. Not that I could ever replace what Chas took onto the field, but I could help in other ways.

*The old Pavilion at the point of demolition.
Picture Courtesy of Eric Ludlow.*

Before I arrived, that characterful but splintery old cricket pavilion had been replaced by a new-build state of the art pavilion, as good as any club pavilion you could wish for. A tremendous effort in fundraising was made by the whole club, I came down from Buxton to a couple of such events. That said, the driving force behind the new pavilion, and the club as a whole, was the club chairman Major Brian Short, a man worthy of his own book. There will be few people reading this who didn't at one time or another have a serious disagreement with Brian (I know I did) or at the very least felt quite opposed to his opinion. None more so than when it came to playing the game, Brian would pronounce on the game like an unmarried Marriage Guidance Counsellor.

Inside the old pavilion Warminster, at the back brother Chas, Front left Graham 'Tubby' Prince next to The Maj. Mr Brian Short. Extreme right at the front Eric Ludlow. Picture Courtesy of Eric Ludlow.

The old pavilion Warminster with Eric Ludlow (or is it James Bond?) The Maj is seated by the door.
Picture courtesy of Eric Ludlow.

I remember being told some years ago that the trouble with ex-army people is that they'd spent their entire lives either telling people what to do or, being told what to do. I think there is little doubt that the Maj. came from the former, but what cannot be understated about the man was his terrific love for the club and its people. Ex-army or not he was a successful businessman and that acumen was brought to the running of Warminster Cricket Club. Whether it was his idea or not (probably John Baldwins'?), the installation of a Skittles Alley in the clubroom of the new pavilion was genius. It meant the pavilion and more importantly the bar was in constant use throughout the winter months, generating enough profit that the club wanted for nothing.

The standing of the club had been enhanced to such a degree that it now felt able, and had the facilities, to accommodate three testimonial matches.

Though not a first-class county itself, Wiltshire did neighbour both Gloucestershire and Somerset, and this being the case, the club played a match against a Gloucestershire XI for Bill Athey. It was a sight to see David 'Syd' Lawrence storming in from the West Parade end.

In the following few seasons, the club hosted Somerset XI's for the testimonials of both Vic Marks and Neil Mallender.

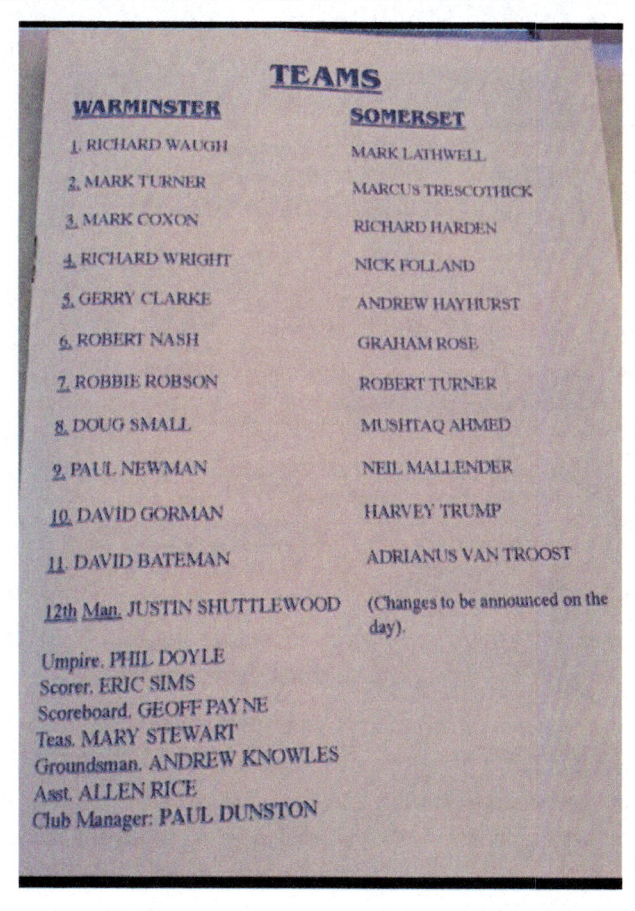

TEAMS

WARMINSTER	SOMERSET
1. RICHARD WAUGH	MARK LATHWELL
2. MARK TURNER	MARCUS TRESCOTHICK
3. MARK COXON	RICHARD HARDEN
4. RICHARD WRIGHT	NICK FOLLAND
5. GERRY CLARKE	ANDREW HAYHURST
6. ROBERT NASH	GRAHAM ROSE
7. ROBBIE ROBSON	ROBERT TURNER
8. DOUG SMALL	MUSHTAQ AHMED
9. PAUL NEWMAN	NEIL MALLENDER
10. DAVID GORMAN	HARVEY TRUMP
11. DAVID BATEMAN	ADRIANUS VAN TROOST
12th Man. JUSTIN SHUTTLEWOOD	(Changes to be announced on the day).

Umpire. PHIL DOYLE
Scorer. ERIC SIMS
Scoreboard. GEOFF PAYNE
Teas. MARY STEWART
Groundsman. ANDREW KNOWLES
Asst. ALLEN RICE
Club Manager: PAUL DUNSTON

I haven't been in the clubhouse for too long but I delight in noticing that it is now the Brian Short Pavilion. Brian passed away a few years ago, but he'll never be forgotten by those members and players at the club who were about when he was.

The magnificent Brian Short pavilion with the indoor nets behind. Picture courtesy of Alex Macdonald.

Brian was very instrumental in one more huge and almost unheard-of development for a provincial cricket club, for at the back of the pavilion, where the club had conventional practice nets, were built state of the art Indoor Nets. This is a massive achievement for a club of Warminster's stature and I've never come across a similar facility at any other club North or South that I have played or officiated at.

Without doubt Warminster was a progressive cricket club, it had a number of excellent young cricketers and there was a desire within the club to move forward and expand. We also had more and more people looking to play cricket. To this end, first team regular and club *tour de force* Colin Webb offered to run and captain a third team in the lower echelons of the Wiltshire league, this was typical of a man still able to compete at the highest level, but putting club first.

Indoor Nets at Warminster.

Colin, to no one's surprise, made a great success of this and the 3's, I think, got a promotion in their first season.

Such were the numbers of potential playing members the club had, coupled with up-and-coming junior players, it was decided that we might run a 4th XI, so I gave up 2nd XI cricket to run the 4ths. This decision was not as charitable as that of Colin's, I knew I wasn't going to play much longer as I really wanted to take the umpiring course and concentrate on that. So, I thought a couple of years to establish a 4th team and then on with the white coat... stick some would say!!

A feature of the club's progression was that the cricketing committee thought that it was high time the club engage a professional. Brian wasn't so sure of this, didn't like the idea much at all. So, somewhat behind his back, I chatted with Colin Webb and explained that I was going to Bristol that week to take Commander Richard Attwater, a local supporter of the club, to see his beloved Gloucestershire take on the South Africans.

I did a little work around Bristol in the morning and got to the ground about twenty minutes before lunch. Richard had left me a ticket at the gate, so I went in and found him sat at a table in front of the pavilion in deep conversation with Mike Proctor. Richard introduced me to Mike and I sat with them. The subsequent conversation I had with Mike Proctor led him to go and fetch the South African tour manager, a man named Fritz Bing. I explained to Mr Bing that I was representing Warminster CC and that we felt it was time we had a club professional. Mr Bing was very enthusiastic and said there were a number of young cricketers he could recommend, he gave me his card and his contact details. I told him I hoped to be in touch after our next meeting back in Warminster.

An aside here, as I sat with the aforementioned people, the umpires lifted the bails for lunch. This was the signal for I don't know how many schoolkids to run on to the pitch and surround the South African fielder, Jonty Rhodes.

I say fielder, Jonty Rhodes was regarded as the best fielder of his generation and by many as the best fielder in the history of the game. He stayed on the pitch signing autographs to the point where his teammates started to return for the afternoon session. At this point he ran off, reappearing in the pavilion doorway a couple of minutes later holding a cup of tea. No sooner was this finished than he was straight back on to join his colleagues.

This would have been South Africa's first tour to England since re-admittance to Test Playing Nation status following Apartheid, what a great ambassador Mr Rhodes was in the re-building of relationships.

Back in Warminster Colin and I had a pint with Brian and I explained what we had done, he still wasn't 100% behind the idea, but he had mellowed a little. I think our nearest rivals in Westbury had engaged an Australian and they/he were doing well and this tempered his resistance to the idea. I gave him Mr Bing's details, 'leave it with me' he said.

The exact details of what happened next are unknown to me,

suffice to say Brian either through the lad at Westbury or of his own accord produced for the club a young Australian called Sean Maxwell.

I've given some thought as to who the best cricketer I've ever played with was. I've obviously discounted the actual first-class professionals such as those I encountered with or against at Buxton, but other than these, I am actually in no doubt that Sean would top that list.

Before I'd ever even seen him play cricket, he was asked if he played golf, 'yeah, a bit' came the reply. So up to West Wilts GC a few of us went, Sean with borrowed clubs. We were teeing it up, trying to whack it miles, no one more so than Dave Stewart who hadn't middled a ball, golf or cricket if it didn't go into at least the next county. Sean took a three iron, threw the ball onto the ground, no wooden or plastic tee, and effortlessly smote it right up the middle. I remember thinking there and then, if he hits a cricket ball like that...

WCC the season Angie and I left Warminster. Sean is 3rd seated with the wicket-keeping kit on. Picture courtesy Sarh Maxwell.

One of the very first games of cricket I watched him play was against Trowbridge, I think it was a cup game but played in the evening, anyhow, Sean was fielding at point, the Trowbridge opening batsman fairly middled one in his direction. Sean made a terrific dive to stop the boundary but, in a flash, while still on his knees, he threw the wicket down, thus running out said batsman. I had never seen a batsman more gobsmacked, he just stood looking around him as if to say what happened there, to be honest I think most of the Warminster fielders had exactly the same reaction. Such fielding from a club cricketer I'd never seen before and I've played with some good ones, Martin Jackson, Noddy Forder, Nick Smith, Doug Small to name but four spring to mind, all very good, but this was a different level again.

Of course, Sean batted like a dream, could keep wicket, bowl anything and catch pigeons. The club employed him to do a little coaching but mostly as the groundsman, which he took to like a duck to water and had the place looking immaculate and the pitches excellent.

I think without any shadow of a doubt Sean singlehandedly raised the performance level of the 1st XI and the team became a formidable outfit.

Perhaps three or four times thanks to my great friend Robert Waller, I guested for the Balliol cricket team. Once or twice in Oxford at the beautiful Masters Field ground of the college.

Who would have thought an ordinary bloke from the north could play amongst the dreaming spires, for a college that had thus far provided us with four Prime Ministers, but a college that came across less elitist than the organisers of the Derbyshire Schoolboy cricket team.

On one occasion, to help make up the numbers, I took Sean with me to the beautiful ground of Downside School in the shadow of the magnificent Downside Abbey, set in the attractive countryside of East Somerset.

I don't recall the outcome of the match but do remember a stunning knock of 80 by Sean, and a comment from one of our team members that, 'we had the better professional', as the Downside 'Ravens' team, mainly made up of teachers with the occasional monk, had a young South African pro as cricket coach.

Levels were somehow raised throughout the whole club and in one *annus mirabilis* (though I can't remember which, perhaps '95 or '96?) the 1st XI won the Wiltshire League Premier division and all the other three teams either won or gained promotion from their respective divisions.

For our annual dinner that year the committee decided we needed a special speaker, I suggested Bill Frindall the Test Match Special scorer as he was a noted after dinner speaker and lived in Wiltshire at Urchfont near Devizes.

I made contact with him by faxing (that makes this sound like ancient history) the TMS team at the BBC, explaining the seasons achievements of the club and would he be available. Within a couple of days, I got a reply saying he would be delighted to speak at our dinner. He was talking at a luncheon in Bath the same day, so would take the train to Warminster. The only addition to his normal fee would be that the club provide him a taxi home to Urchfont.

He certainly didn't let us down doing some of his famous impersonations, John Arlott and Fred Trueman, and handing out the club awards for that year. Mr Frindall then presented the club with a beautiful print of the Wagon Wheel shot map of Brian Lara's 375 scored against England at Antigua in 1994.

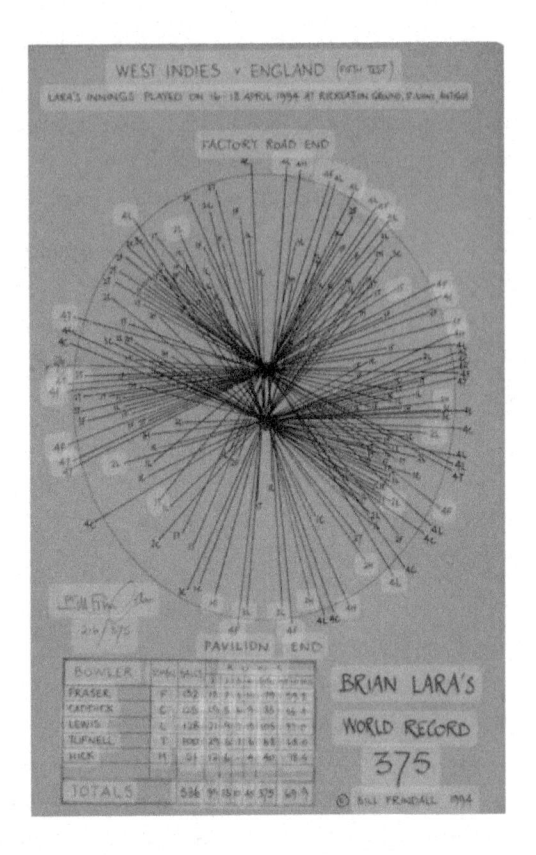

It was quite a novel thing for me to join a cricket club that had a steward, but the addition of the Skittle Alley and 365-day opening meant that the need was inevitable.

Mary and Neville Stewart, Dave and Mickey (not the Surrey legend!) Stewart's mum and dad were the stewards when we first moved to Warminster, but before long we got Dunners.

If two old Yorkshire codgers were talking to each other about Paul Dunstan, one would lean into the other and whisper, 'ee bats f' t'other side tha knows'.

That aside, Paul was one of those -once met never forgot- people who was a fantastic addition to the cricket club. Very knowledgeable with a great humour, decent culinary skills, kept a very passable pint and didn't suffer fools. He was a joy, and to watch him and Brian Short joust was pure theatre.

Paul would also do a few odd jobs around the pavilion. It was said, (now I didn't see this so it might be a myth) that a soap holder was knocked off the shower wall and Paul, in his impish, mischievous manner, re-affixed said soap holder just six inches off the floor...

Thinking about Warminster CC after 25 years away is testing my memory bones and one of the things that comes first into my head is a chap who played for us who was in the army, he was I think of Sri Lankan heritage and his name was Anil Nahasapeemapetilon. (Not really, that second name is Apu in the Simpsons - I can't find anyone who can remember Anil's actual second name).

Anyway, sometime before my arrival in the delightful town of Warminster, it was decided to build some houses adjacent to the boundary that ran from the pavilion to the scorebox. The club or builders, or both, built a generous wire mesh fence, at least two times if not more, higher than say a tennis court fence might be. In addition to this the club added further netting to the top of the wire fence, so in total there was quite a barrier of some height protecting the new houses.

Nothing is 100% effective and the odd ball did go over and, maybe twice in my 11 years a window got broke or a tile smashed. Whenever this happened the club immediately took remedial action, no questions asked.

The incident I recall was when a ball did not go over the fence but got stuck in the top netting. We had no ladders or anything long enough to knock it down with, but when Anil appeared on the scene, he took one look at the ball nestling high in the netting and without giving it a second thought, walked up the fence like it was lying on the ground. It's hard to do it justice but his incredible athleticism and fearlessness got him to the top, he shook the ball loose, and back down he came in the same free and easy manner in which he went up. I know of no one who could have done that in the way that Anil did, it seemed utterly effortless.

I now think that what reminded of this story was watching the climbing events at the 2024 Paris Olympics, Anil went up that fence with the same ease those climbers attack that wall.

I spent a couple of years looking after the ground but never did I have looking so immaculate as David Bateman now has it. Picture courtesy Alex MacDonald.

There were another couple of cricketing adventures while at Warminster, having always been a keen 'Tourist' a few of us thought that Warminster CC on tour sounded like a good scheme.

So, our first effort at a tour was to Shrewsbury, not a totally memorable affair apart from a couple of exceptions.

We played a fixture at the beautiful ground of Bewdley CC on the way up to Shrewsbury, sadly this was the only good day's weather we enjoyed, I don't recall much other cricket but we had a lot of fun on a par 3 golf course. One other memory imprinted on my brain is of a Karaoke evening back at the hotel. We had devised a system of punishment for the inevitable bad singing, where every soft drink we could think of was put in one hat and every spirit we could think of in another.

When it came to Dave Stewart's go and he'd butchered Freddie Mercury, I vividly remember him having to down a Bailey's and Tomato Juice, and in typical DS fashion he did so, in one, with gusto.

(Answers on a postcard if you can think of a more disgusting concoction) Dave was another friend sadly taken too soon.

So, where to go next, well where better than my old stomping ground of Buxton, for one thing it would be a tour I could easily arrange. Not within my remit however was the weather. Little cricket was played, though we did start the match against Buxton, much to the chagrin of Ravi Aylesbury who nicked the first ball of the tour to slip. It seems a little cruel to mention this but it did take half a dozen of us three days to stop laughing.

It's funny how you live in a place for thirty-three years and yet somebody who has only been there for one day can tell you something you never knew. Namely, and I was advised of this by local Warminster heartthrob and ***** magnet Nat Davies, that all Buxton women were lesbians! (This came as a great surprise to me!)

That afternoon in the Buxton pavilion a challenge was laid down to see who could down a pint the quickest. Warminster had its own champion in Phil Doyle, (more of whom later) I wasn't involved in the arrangements, but I'm guessing someone asked Phil to name his drink of choice, so as you do, Phil decided on red wine. Two pints of red wine appeared, and Phil's disappeared almost as quickly.

Have you noticed there is a theme to cricket tours ....

Having returned to my old stomping ground, Colin Webb took up the mantle and arranged the next tour to his, Southend. Never have I seen a tide go so far out, I toyed with the idea that the hotel I'd put us in the year before in Buxton, was actually nearer to the sea than the one Colin had put us in in Southend... but their Pier was longer.

I'm sure the weather was better and cricket was played but my two abiding memories of this tour have nothing to do with the reason we were there.

Golf, as ever, was on the agenda. I didn't play In Southend but enjoyed a walk around the course. I suddenly came across a group of my touring colleagues searching some bushes and thick shrubbery, 'Whose ball is it?' I asked, but was laughingly informed that they weren't looking for a ball but Nat Davies's putter! Clearly Nat had missed a sitter, and lost a little patience.

My other memory of this tour was of sharing a room with Phil Meadows.

Phil snored like a cartoon dog; I swear the duvet he was under lifted six inches with every adenoidal exhalation. Either that or he was playing a bugle under there - not a euphemism....

Our next tour was instigated by a player who had come to join us from Sussex. Richard Wright was a police officer who had played for Three Bridges CC in Crawley.

So off we all toddled to our hotel on the front in Brighton. Fixtures followed at Three Bridges and at the beautiful Ardingly CC, plus others I just can't remember. The cricket I remember little of, but I do recall eating the most delicious Italian food in a restaurant in The Lanes, courtesy of my good friend Robert who had joined us for this trip.

I think yet again, a number of us somewhat overenthusiastically took advantage of the services offered by the late-night bar in the hotel.

I now realise having got to this part of my touring recollections that we also went to Southport on tour. My memory doesn't allow that we went to Lancashire before the Buxton trip or after, just not sure. But we did enjoy a few nights in the excellent Scarisbrick Hotel on Lord Street.

Fixtures would have been arranged by Paul Edwards who has become a good friend who I met when he was studying at Oxford at the same time as Robert.

We had a game at the splendid Trafalgar Road home of Southport and Birkdale CC, a ground used by Lancashire for first class matches.

Southport is the centre of the Golf Coast of England, containing no fewer than 11 of the top 100 courses to be found here. None more famous than the Royal Birkdale which has hosted The Open ten times. So, yet again on this trip we played as much golf, if not more, than cricket.

We hadn't been in Warminster very long, 1989, when another unique cricketing opportunity arose.

My good friend Robert Waller (he of the little yellow cricket bat of my youth) had been asked by Sir Patrick Mayhew if he could rustle up a President's XI to play against Kilndown CC, the Kent village club that Sir Patrick was president of, as well as being the local M.P.

So, taking a Saturday off club cricket, Angela and I pootled across the south of England and found ourselves enjoying the Pantiles area of Royal Tunbridge Wells, a nice walk round, possibly/probably a glass of something and a pleasant nosebag. Then off to the village of Kilndown and our digs for the night, a very cordial pub on the corner of the cricket ground named the 'Globe and Rainbow'.

A very agreeable buffet lunch provided by Sir Patrick followed on the Sunday before play commenced.

On this occasion the cricket was most memorable as my good friend Paul Edwards - he of the Southport tour - took nine wickets in the Kilndown innings, I took the other one.

A great weekend away.

The evidence of Mr Edwards' flight and guile.

I am at number four on the back row standing next to Sir Patrick Mayhew. My friend of 65 years, Robert Waller is on the end of the bench scratching his beard. He had managed to top score on the day with 77. Next to him is another friend and contemporary of his from Oxford, Peter Andrews. At number two on the back row is the hero of the day, Paul Edwards.

Thinking now about my days in Warminster I feel genuinely blessed to have been part of such a great club, the camaraderie, friendships, the craic, (as we say here in Ireland) the dramas, but most of all the warm, welcoming and friendly people.

A great club and a great place to play cricket.

I didn't want to end this section on Warminster C.C. without mentioning another kind soul who sadly, is no longer with us.

When I was doing a little coaching of the juniors at the club, a young lad attended who, though not blessed with the most natural of techniques, was desperate to improve and showed terrific dedication to just that.

Nobody asked more questions about how, or why, or what am I doing wrong than Graham Few. It was a real pleasure that Graham became proficient enough to play 2nd, 3rd or 4th team matches with me and whichever side he was in, Graham always gave 100%.

Above all else though, Graham was an out and out Saints fan. If Southampton F.C. was his church, then for Graham, (and many, many other Saints fans) Matt Le Tissier was his god. He kept on talking to me about taking me to the Dell, so in August 1995 I succumbed. On a Wednesday night, Graham drove me to his beloved Dell to watch the Premier League fixture with Leeds United. The great Matt did play but, on this occasion, didn't score, that privilege went to Tommy Widdrington who put the Saints ahead. Sadly, for Graham, Tony Dorigo levelled for the visitors and the match finished 1-1.

When Angela and I left Warminster in 1999, Graham would have been just 22 and thriving in the farm work he loved.

So, it came as a profound shock, in May 2019, to be advised that Graham had died, at home, at the desperately young age of 42, leaving behind a wife and family.

The ancient Greeks had it: *"Whom the Gods love, die young."*

UMPIRING

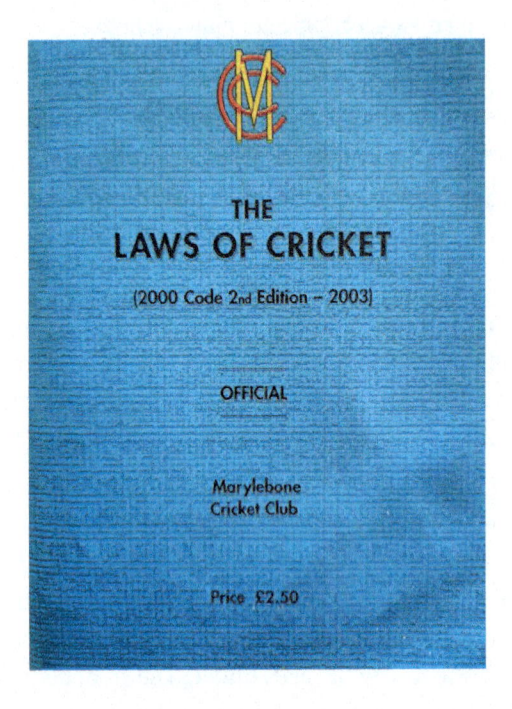

Having arrived at that point in my playing career where I just hurt too much on a Sunday morning, and also coming to the realisation that my sporting physique was now less Racing Snake more Python that had swallowed a Pig, I decided it was time to don the white coat and get paid for turning up on a Saturday afternoon rather than it costing a fortune.

So, with a friend from Warminster C.C. we enrolled on a winter umpiring course that was being held in Salisbury. Now, I have indicated the size I had got to, well my friend Phil (Pint of Red Wine) could, at the time, give me about five stones. Even though there were only two of us sat in my little red Golf, such was the pressure of weight we generated, the front of the car must have still been slightly raised as we were constantly flashed by oncoming traffic both to and from Salisbury each week.

What a joy those weekly trips to Salisbury were. A number of existing umpires took the course with a number of aides provided by the Umpires association. We went week by week through all 42 Laws of the game. (If asked, always say there are 43 Laws. Law 43 says that any occurrence not covered in the first 42 should be dealt with by common sense). Of course, you think you know the laws until you actually start to learn them. I think I may have, (under my breath) erroneously said some very derogatory things about umpires who were standing while I was bowling.

In my playing days I would invariably open the bowling and would often try to lighten the mood with the umpire by saying something like, 'Welcome Umps and just to help you, I'll only appeal if it's out'.

After a number of weeks' study I soon realised that I might not have been always right.

On we forged, Phil and I, and it wasn't always easy, we were constantly told that a good knowledge of all 42 Laws would be required for the exam and whilst we knew there would definitely be some questions around the LBW and No Ball Laws, all the other questions could pertain to any of the other 40. As it turns out we both passed and enjoyed a good few years arbitrating on Saturday afternoons.

For my sins, I joined the 'Bristol and West Cricket Umpires and Scorers Association' it was something like that anyway, but it meant I could officiate in the highest level of league cricket in the area at that time, the Western League. This league was swallowed up in the ECB re-organisation of club cricket throughout England and Wales. It is now part of the ECB West of England Premier League, this incorporates the very best clubs in Somerset, Bristol, Gloucestershire and Wiltshire into a pyramid structure.

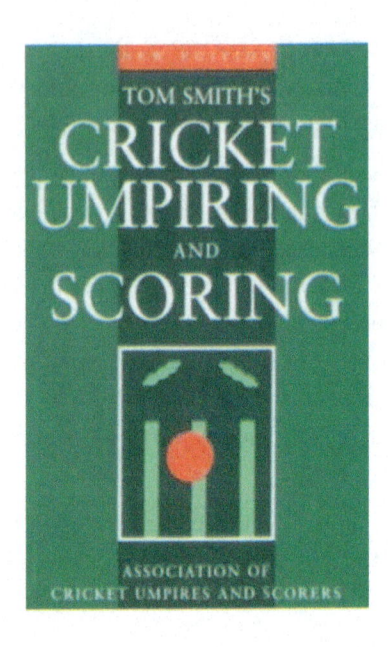

One of my early appointments was at Lansdown Cricket Club in Bath. A very good cricket club indeed, I believe it's where Viv Richards played when he first came to England before joining up with Somerset. Anyway, when you stand at Lansdown, a club official gives you a bleeper with the instruction that if it goes off, to quickly retrieve the stumps and leave the playing area.

After about an hour into the game, my bleeper and that of my colleague started to vibrate with a dull ringing sound. We both gathered the stumps at our respective ends and followed the players off to the dressing room. I think before we'd even reached the clubhouse, we could hear the Air Ambulance circling above before dropping to land on the outfield of the ground, which gave access to the Royal United Hospital Bath Emergency Entrance.

We watched from a distance as a stretcher was removed from the ambulance and placed onto a gurney that had been wheeled out of the hospital to meet it. The whole operation was very efficient, within seconds of landing the patient was being taken in to A&E and only a couple of minutes or so later the helicopter was airborne again and we proceeded to restart the game.

Being now a 'proper' umpire, I had of course confirmed the time of leaving and returning to the field with my colleague, as we would have to agree with all timings for the report card we would have to sign after the match.

One of the advantages of umpiring at this level was that you saw, from very close range, the best players club cricket had to offer and the Western League was as good as any.

I recall a number of good knocks and terrific bowling spells but one delivery stands out in my memory more than any other.

This was at Frome, who were bowling first, I think against Knowle CC from South Bristol. Frome had a bowler, who though quite short in stature was really quite quick, his name was Billy Blacklidge and I had never come across him before or since. He bowled a delivery to the Knowle opening batsman that was a perfect length, pitched two inches outside the off stump and completely uprooted the middle peg from about two inches below the bail. Billy obviously never saw me bat and after the back slapping and congratulations he received from his team-mates had finished, I said to him, 'Would've probably got me out that one'.

The one great advantage to retiring from playing is that you immediately become a much better player.

One sadness to me is that I'd been asked to umpire in an early season friendly fixture between Wiltshire and the Army. The game was to be played at the Tidworth Garrison and I was really looking forward to it.

However, after accepting the appointment with great anticipation, another opportunity arose.

At about the same time I would have been calling 'Play' at Tidworth, I was actually pulling a pint or two in the Golden Ball Inn, Lower Swell, a pub that Angela and I had taken on, it was attached to the same brewery that brother Chas was with, about two miles away from his.

This book isn't about that, but suffice to say what with a petrol crisis and then the Foot and Mouth epidemic, running a country pub was not the easiest of occupations and after two years we left.

However, before we left a situation presented itself that was just too good to miss.

Even though I was taking a break from umpiring I had continued with my membership of the Umpires Association. I received notification that the next Annual General Meeting of the association would be held in the Long Room at Lords cricket ground.

This was a wonderful opportunity to visit hallowed ground, and I was sure I would never be in such a position again. So, early one Saturday morning I drove to Kingham station, boarded the train to Paddington, made a short underground journey and alighted at St. Johns Wood.

Once at the ground I had a few minutes to kill, so I took the opportunity to have a walk around and found myself gazing up at the new Media Centre building at the Nursery End of the ground.

The Lords Media Centre. Picture: Alamy stock photo.

Suddenly a voice at my shoulder asked, "What do you think?" I replied, "I like it... I think". "Yes," came the response, "it gets you a bit like that at first, but I like it." I then turned to see who my interlocutor was and I was little surprised to see that I was talking to Ted Dexter, once a hero of that parish. I never saw him play at anything like his best but clearly remember him commentating for the BBC. Then he became Chairman of Selectors in a time of somewhat upheaval in English cricket.

He was very pleasant with me that morning, and as we walked back, we would walk up to the playing area between the seated sections and take in the view of the ground on offer, from these different angles Mr Dexter would regale me with one anecdote or another that the view re-awakened. I wish I could remember them, but can't, suffice to say that the whole experience was a most pleasant surprise. Mr Dexter wished me well, said some very pleasant things about the job umpires did and disappeared out through the Grace Gates.

The A.G.M. was much the same as any other, voting on a few resolutions and re-electing officers and committees etc, though it was made a tad different by the view I had, sat on a highchair looking out at perhaps the most famous vista in cricket.

If the move from playing cricket in Derbyshire to that of Wiltshire, was a bit of a culture shock, then the move to cricket in Yorkshire, more particularly South Yorkshire was an even greater one, though not necessarily as pleasant. Not that it was awful, but it was often jarring, inharmonious, teams showed the respect for one another as football teams would. In the lower divisions a whitish Leeds Utd shirt would do as cricket Whites, against the express regulations of the League, but it was often argued it was that kit or no game, insufficient numbers, invoke Law 43.

What really struck me when we moved to Doncaster was the sheer volume of cricket teams and leagues in Yorkshire. In Doncaster there were at least two other leagues the smaller clubs might play in, not counting some very popular evening leagues. The

South Yorkshire Cricket League had nine divisions.

Just to give you some idea, I once read that there were as many leagues in Yorkshire, as there were clubs in Wiltshire, or many other counties.

The standard at the top of the SYCL was very good, as good as anywhere I had stood, the second and third divisions would also be a very satisfactory and enjoyable level to stand in. But, nine divisions meant perhaps 90 teams which in turn required 90 umpires and there were of course, never that many. The top two, and probably the third division would be allocated two umpires but after that you would be lucky to have a partner to stand with, so that was most of the time. To be fair to the league, there was no favouritism towards umpires, in that during the course of a season you might get to stand in each division twice. So, six Saturdays could be really looked forward to, most of the others might be harder work.

I didn't mind standing at both ends, you got one and a half fees as it were and were never out of the game, but it did have its moments.

I recall standing at one of the Sheffield clubs, where the home teams elderly off break bowler was giving it a fair tweak, every ball was spinning down the leg side and the hapless batsman, trying to hit with the spin, missed it every time. On the last ball of one of these overs - the batsman having played and missed five times - the bowler, turning to go back to his mark, winked at me. I knew what was coming, the bowler delivered the next ball as straight as a dye, imparting no spin on the ball whatsoever, the batsman getting more and more frustrated with every missed delivery, once more stepped back and across to hit it to leg. He of course missed it and the ball hit his pad just in front of middle stump. A loud appeal followed by the raising of my finger. As the disgruntled batsman walked off past me he said, 'fuckin ell umpire, couldn't tha see how far 'e wa' turnin' it'. Not all Yorkshiremen know all about cricket.

But some do...

Towards the end of my time umpiring in South Yorkshire, I stood in a game at Sheffield Collegiate CC. The home team opening batsman scored a very good hundred and during his innings he told me that the lad in the score box returning my signals was his son. The batsman's name was Matt Root...

(I can't be definite but this was probably Joe who would have been 10 or 11 at the time, Billy is a couple of years younger.)

At one of the ex-mining communities on the edge of Doncaster, a pit village similar to the one Angie and I lived in, was a team that played in one of the lower divisions. Like a lot of such grounds, I assume it was the Pit/Miners Welfare ground prior to the pit closures. The pavilion area with bowling greens attached would have been the Pit Club. The playing area was half decent though grass pitches had been done away with in favour of a maintenance free artificial one. When standing at the pavilion end you were enchanted by the spray-painted message, in black, that 'tim fuked lucy'. (Who knows, perhaps while Tim should have been in an English class?).

Also, you were required to bring the stumps and bails in with you at the tea interval, for fear there might be a post prandial deficit.

While I have never lost my love for the great game of cricket, there did come a point, whilst umpiring in South Yorkshire, that I was becoming a little less enamoured with my Saturdays.

Standing at both ends, which was fun at first, was becoming a little tiring and exasperating. Certainly, in the lower divisions the behaviour of some of the teams, even some captains, was becoming more and more churlish, and I found that I was not enjoying it as much as I used to.

We also had at home a very big garden which my green fingered wife had big designs on, but needed my help with the heavy lifting and landscaping. So, I swapped the white coat for a wheelbarrow and a whole heap of brownie points.

***

I have come to realise that in my seventy years on this planet my happiest and most joyful moments (family apart) have been realised by being a part of the club cricket scene.

Club cricket has given me friends too numerous to list but all equally treasured.

What club cricket does, and brings to any community, is inclusion and the opportunity to become part of something. It enables social connection, recreation, fitness (some get more of this than others!) camaraderie, a sense of belonging and team spirit and dare I say it a competitive edge.

I think of all these beneficial attributes the most important is inclusion. Not just the fact that so many cricket clubs now have a Ladies Playing Section, which is to be welcomed and embraced but, as my dedication list suggests, all ages, sizes, shapes and abilities are welcome into the cricket club family.

If cricket is a metaphor for life, then the people I've met along the way are its finest lesson.

Thank you for sharing this innings with me. Until we meet again, in cricket or elsewhere, may your skies be clear and your pitches true.

And the bar be open...

SOME OTHER PHOTOGRAPHS

Alan Burgess, Chas, Cec, the author and Peter Cockram at the erecting of the Pavilion Clock in remembrance of our Mum and Dad.

TIMELY MEMORIES

TWO supporters of Buxton Cricket Club will be remembered for a long time to come thanks to a clock donated in their memory by their sons.

Bill Knowles was a player, chairman, vice-president and life member and his wife Olive was for many years an active member of the ladies' section.

Pictured with the pavilion clock are first team captain Alan Burgess (left), Charles, Cecil and Andrew Knowles and chairman Peter Cochrane (right). The clock was built and erected by W.J. Fry and Son.

Chas taking a turn with the scorebook, a very young John Bond and Roger Davey looking on.

The Welsh Pony, Oxford.

The following poem was written by the author after a non-too-successful day in the Derbyshire Cup at Heanor.

John Duddy was an excellent cricketer with bat and ball, but he had a particularly bad day on Sunday 18th July 1982...

He was not by the way a man of the cloth (though he looked like one) but worked as a representative for Marstons Brewery alongside his good mate Brian Jackson.

John had one other claim to uniqueness, he was the only person I played with who had a Colostomy Bag. Consequently, he is also the only person I ever heard, when running into bowl, stop, put his hand up, and say: 'Sorry batsman, I'm just having a shit'...'

It became fashionable for a time, at Buxton, to replace the word Head with Shed, so instead of saying 'His head's collapsed' or 'He's gone in the head' we would say 'shed', don't ask me why it's just one of those things.

(To be sung in the style of Lord Kitchener or any of those great Calypsonians.)

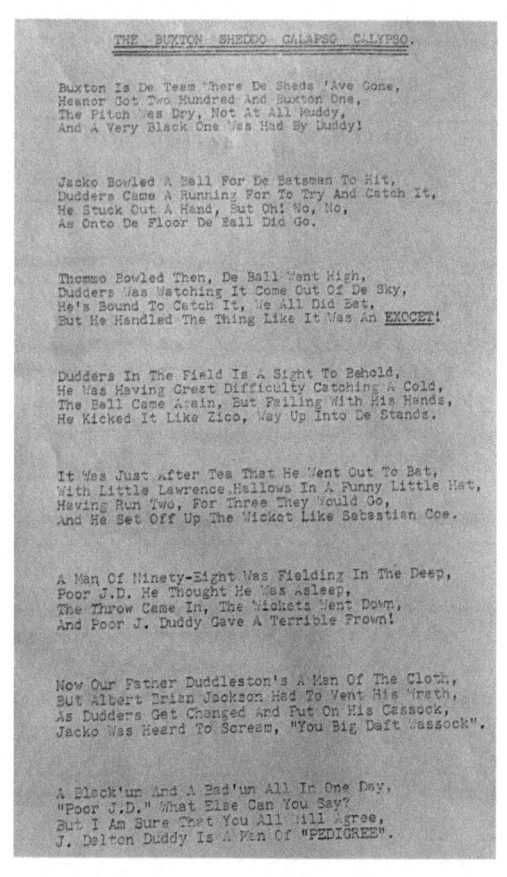

```
THE BUXTON SHEDDO CALAPSO CALYPSO.

Buxton Is De Team There De Sheds 'Ave Gone,
Heanor Got Two Hundred And Buxton One,
The Pitch Was Dry, Not At All Muddy,
And A Very Black One Was Had By Duddy!

Jacko Bowled A Ball For De Batsman To Hit,
Dudders Came A Running For To Try And Catch It,
He Stuck Out A Hand, But Oh! No, No,
As Onto De Floor De Ball Did Go.

Thommo Bowled Then, De Ball Went High,
Dudders Was Watching It Come Out Of De Sky,
He's Bound To Catch It, We All Did Bet,
But He Handled The Thing Like It Was An EXOCET!

Dudders In The Field Is A Sight To Behold,
He Was Having Great Difficulty Catching A Cold,
The Ball Came Again, But Failing With His Hands,
He Kicked It Like Zico, Way Up Into De Stands.

It Was Just After Tea That He Went Out To Bat,
With Little Lawrence Hallows In A Funny Little Hat,
Having Run Two, For Three They Would Go,
And He Set Off Up The Wicket Like Sebastian Coe.

A Man Of Ninety-Eight Was Fielding In The Deep,
Poor J.D. He Thought He Was Asleep,
The Throw Came In, The Wickets Went Down,
And Poor J. Duddy Gave A Terrible Frown!

Now Our Father Duddleston's A Man Of The Cloth,
But Albert Brian Jackson Had To Vent His Wrath,
As Dudders Get Changed And Put On His Cassock,
Jacko Was Heard To Scream, "You Big Daft Wassock".

A Black'un And A Bad'un All In One Day,
"Poor J.D." What Else Can You Say?
But I Am Sure That You All Will Agree,
J. Dalton Duddy Is A Man Of "PEDIGREE".
```

Resurrected Courtesy Geoff 'Nudger' Needham.

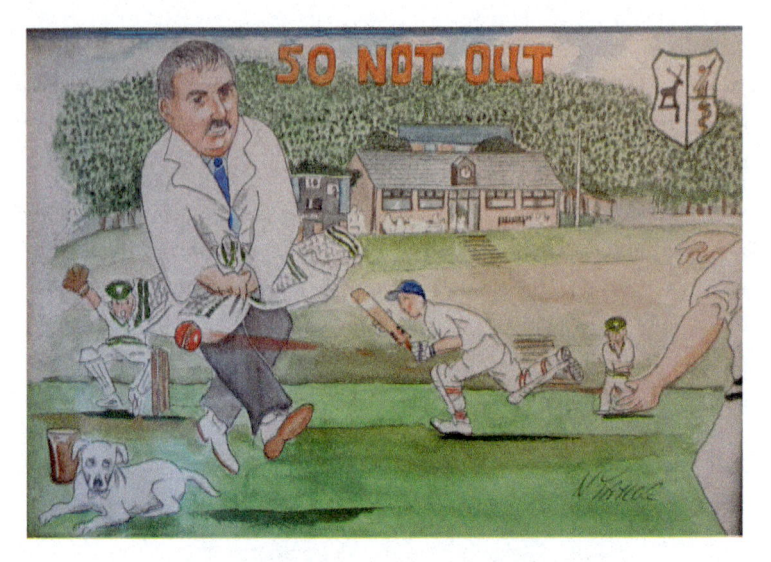

A treasured 50th birthday gift.

ACKNOWLEDGEMENTS

It goes without saying that this book could not have been written without the help of others. Though I must give special mention to Geoff 'Nudger' Needham and Matthew Poole of Buxton CC and Billy Johnson of Warminster without whose patience at being bombarded with questions would mean I was still on page 5.

Billy Johnson
Eric Ludlow
Andrew Pinnell
Geoffrey 'Nudger' Needham
Alan Burgess
Julian Burgess
Paul Drew.
Andrew Drennan
Robyn Hardman
Matthew Poole
Stephen Mycock.
Derbyshire County Cricket Archive.
Chas Knowles
Cec Knowles
Robert Waller
Lea Green Outdoor Activities Centre.
Coates and Parker
Salisbury and Avon Gazette
Matthew Engel
Sarah Maxwell
Peter Andrews
Kevin Beswick
Billy Khan
Edwina Buczynski
Alex MacDonald

Picture courtesy Steve Ormsby.

Andrew Knowles and his wife Angela moved to Ireland in 2017 and now reside in County Roscommon overlooking the mighty River Shannon.

Andrew has written one other book, *Blow Ins* and edited the book *Shannonside Tales.*

A cricket lover since he can remember, this is his story.

arknowles@hotmail.co.uk

Printed in Great Britain
by Amazon